THE SAAS SALES METHOD

SALES AS A SCIENCE

Jacco van der Kooij and Fernando Pizarro

with Dominique Levin and Dan Smith

Copyright © 2021. Published by Winning by Design LLC, a Delaware Company
All rights reserved as permitted under the United States Copyright Act of
1976. No part of this book may be reproduced, used or distributed in any form
or by any means, without expressed written consent of the publisher. The
contents of this book were created in the United States of America.

Revision 3.2

Winning By Design LLC
650 Castro Street, Suite 120-252
Mountain View, CA 94041

Let us see sales renewed,

filled with excitement,

with beautiful purpose,

a professional trade.

                        Jacco J. van der Kooij

WHY YOU SHOULD READ THIS BOOK

This book was written for anyone who works with customers. It is based on a scientific understanding of how revenue generation works in a recurring revenue business. That revenue generation model poses the same questions for the CEO as well as for those in sales, marketing, and customer success: How do I grow the business? How do I get my team to perform? Should I hire more people? Why are my customers churning? Should I run more campaigns? Should I buy more leads? This book will give you the answers to these questions and much more.

This book contains insights gained from working with over 300 companies over a span of four years. Many of them are early-stage, high-tech startups but the list also contains some of the largest companies in the world. The insights we found are the same across all of them:

1. A maniacal focus on new logo acquisition versus generating profits from existing customers.
2. The first response when targets are missed is to blame the people, not to inspect the process.
3. Absence of a uniform methodology across all roles dedicated to the recurring business model.
4. Little understanding of the unit economics that make a recurring business work.
5. Inadequate depth of basic sales skills; everyone is looking for tricks/hacks and shortcuts.

We provide simple answers to address all of the issues. With the knowledge in this book, we aim to enable you to have a strategic conversation in the boardroom, a one-on-one talk with a 30-year sales veteran on the changes in selling, discuss a new LeadGen initiative with the marketing manager, or coach a customer success manager on how to upsell a customer. It's all here. This book was written so the chapters can be read in any order. Page through it and if you see a visual you like, dive in; that's your starting point.

TABLE OF CONTENTS

CHAPTER 1	SCIENCE OVER SUPERSTARS	10
CHAPTER 2	CHANGES IN B2B SALES	22
CHAPTER 3	THE SAAS SALES METHODOLOGY	38
CHAPTER 4	THE SCIENCE	50
CHAPTER 5	MOMENTS THAT MATTER	64
CHAPTER 6	BLUEPRINTS	76
CHAPTER 7	HOW TO KEEP GOING	100
APPENDIX	A FEW HELPFUL TOOLS	106

ABBREVIATIONS USED

ACL	Average Contract Length	MAS	Marketing Automation System
ACE	Appreciate, Check time, set End goal	MDR	Marketing Development Representative
ACV	Annual Contract Value	MQL	Marketing Qualified Lead
AE	Account Executive	MRR	Monthly Recurring Revenue
AM	Account Manager	MTM	Moment That Matters
ARR	Annual Recurring Revenue	ORG	Organization
B2B	Business to Business	PM	Product Manager
B2C	Business to Consumer	POC	Proof Of Concept
BDR	Business Development Representative	RFP	Request For Proposal
CAC	Client Acquisition Cost	RFQ	Request For Quotation
CR	Conversion Ratio	RRR	Relevance, Reward, Request
CRM	Customer Relationship Management	RoI	Return on Investment
CSM	Customer Success Manager	SaaS	Software as a Service
CE	Critical Event	SAAS	Sales As A Science
CEO	Chief Executive Officer	SAL	Sales Accepted Lead
CRO	Chief Revenue Officer	SC	Sales Cycle
CCO	Chief Customer Officer	SDR	Sales Development Representative
DEMO	Demonstration	SE	Sales Engineer
DG	Demand Generation	SKO	Sales Kick-Off
FAE	Field Account Executive	SMB	Small to Medium Business
FFF	Feel, Felt, Found	SQL	Sales Qualified Lead (same as opportunity)
FSR	Field Sales Rep (AE with 80% travel)	VPM	VP of Marketing
ICE	Impact and Critical Event	VPS	VP of Sales
ISR	Inside Sales Rep (same as an AE)	WWW	Who? Why? What's in it for me?
LTV	Lifetime Value of a client	WR	Win Ratio

CHAPTER 1
SCIENCE OVER SUPERSTARS

Many business functions, from operations to marketing, have changed from being driven by intuition and individual contributors to data and process. In operations, supply chain made the transition to Kaizen, a framework that sets the stage for continuous improvement through scientific rigor. In marketing, the discipline of performance marketing has spread through the function with better attribution and ROI measurement. But other functions have held out, with sales being one of the functions most stuck in the old way of doing things.

It is true that in the last ten years, there are parts of the sales function that have begun the transition. Sales leaders have begun to think in terms of measurability of process and outcomes in certain areas. For instance, measures of efficiency like win rates have become a part of many management dashboards. But until now, those changes have been limited and sales as a discipline has continued to be intuitively managed.

THE NEED FOR SCIENCE

Even in the data-driven world of Software as a Service, or *SaaS*, there are very few companies that use a methodology that manages the end-to-end process of selling as efficiently and effectively as they could. To be efficient and effective, companies *should* standardize the entire customer-facing relationship. That includes marketing, sales, and customer success. They should also add the process necessary to achieve continuous improvement comparable to what has become normal in functions, like supply chain.

To do so, they should rely on science. Yet, *in practice,* the overwhelming majority of sales teams we encounter rely on a few superstar performers who deliver the lion's share of results. When those teams get in trouble, sales leaders first ask "Who can we hire?" to fix the problem rather than "What process can we improve?"

It has always been the case that as organizations reach a certain size, it becomes necessary for them to implement process in order to continue to scale. In fact, much of the functional specialization within the sales function that we describe in this book has been present in mature sales organizations for quite some time.

What has changed today for many companies is most of the revenue comes *after* the initial sale - from upsell, cross-sell or renewals. As a result, coordination between pre-sales, sales, and post-sales resources is more important than ever before. Using a defined process with clear hand-offs and teamwork is often at odds with the superstar culture that made high-growth companies sign up their first customers.

What is a superstar culture? It is one that relies on a few high-achieving individuals in either sales leadership roles or individual contributor roles. These superstars appear to use intuitive judgment gained over decades in their industry. That judgment allows them to make decisions rapidly and automatically based on relatively limited information. The problem with relying on this model is that superstars are expensive and hard to find, and the performance of the system is highly variable.

Because these companies rely on highly variable individual performance, they train only sporadically and do not incorporate discipline and methodology into their operations. When an organization with a superstar culture scales, the entire system becomes unstable. Companies can experience this - not once - but a number of times during their growth.

Early stage startups experience this as "Founder Sales." In the early stage of a company, its founder acts as the sales superstar and closes most, if not all, of the deals. As the first salespeople come onboard, none of them are able to perform on par with the founder who has a lifetime of experience. Founders are almost always highly critical of these early sales hires and churn through several leaders as well as individual contributors.

As a result, it takes more time for the team to grow to its potential than it would have with a scientific approach. This happens early when the company transitions away from founder sales, and then all over again, a few years later as the company positions itself to scale. At firms with a superstar culture, it is quite common for 20% of the team to perform consistently and carry as much as 80% of the company's revenue growth. Companies with this culture try to grow by hiring more superstars rather than focusing on how to scale the performance of the other 80% of the team, the "average" performers.

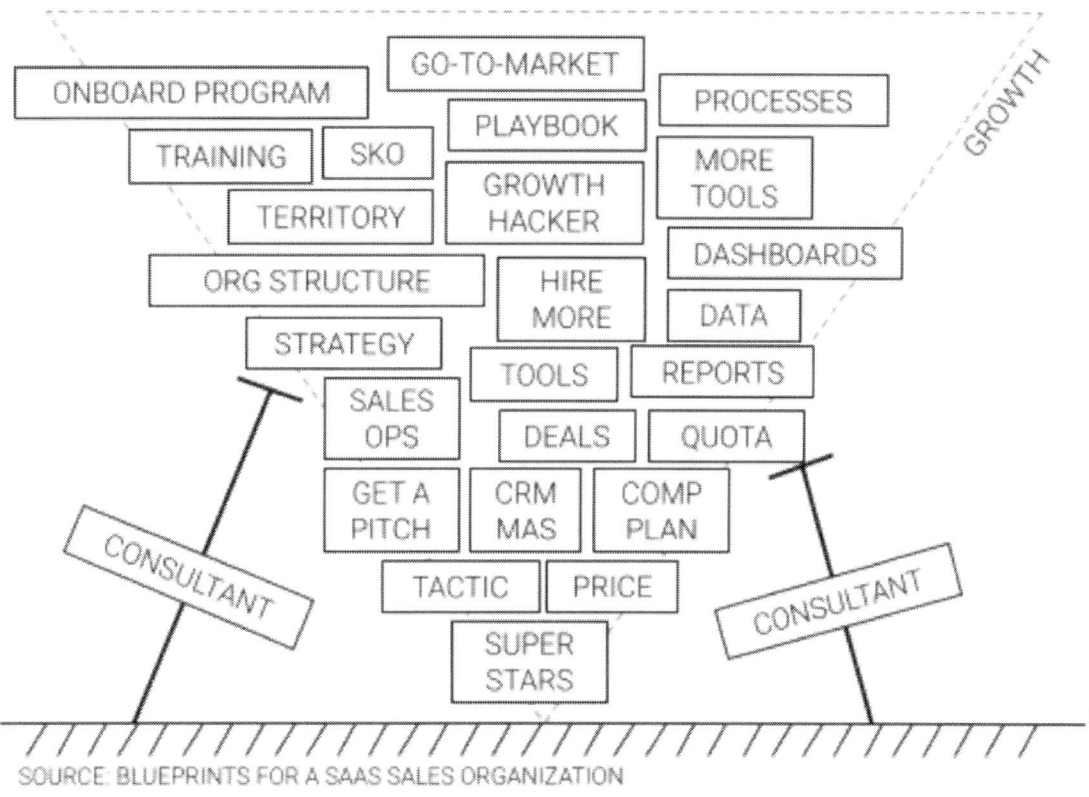

Figure 1.1 In a superstar sales culture, organizations growth with little design

Why not hire more superstars? Superstars are hard to find and even harder to retain. The hiring, retention, and performance of superstars is unpredictable. Most importantly, in the world of land and expand where initial deal sizes are smaller, hiring superstars is no longer an option. No longer can 20% of the team support 80% of the revenues. Instead, successful high-growth companies should make the transition to a science culture to support scaling.

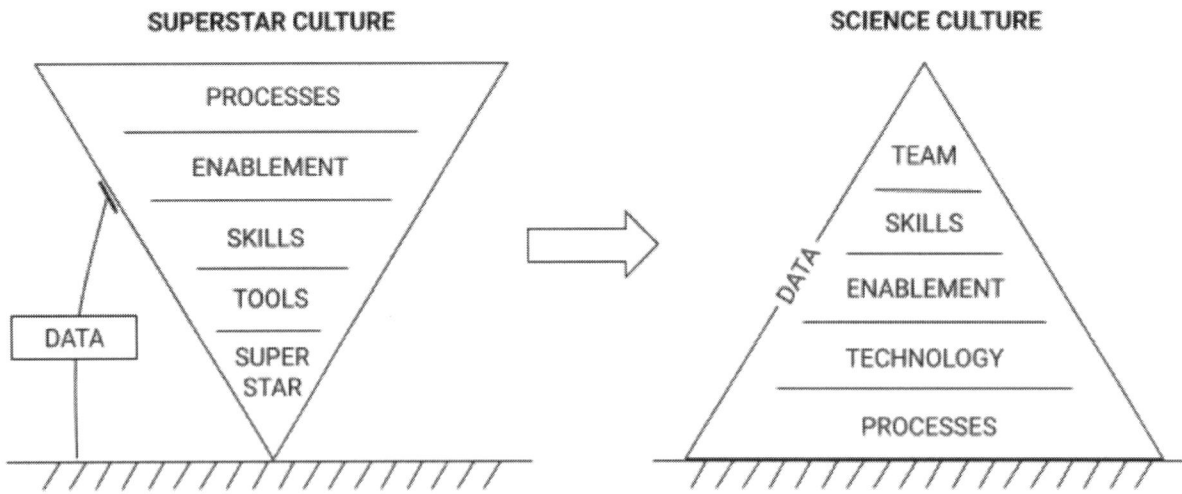

Figure 1.2 Two very different cultures

A science culture focuses on process, technology, enablement, skills and teams.

PROCESSES: In a superstar culture, sales processes are not linked to marketing or customer success. Instead, the sales team operates in a silo. In a science culture, we look closely to coordinate between functions, and for performance gaps in the process to identify opportunities to improve productivity in the most efficient way.

TECHNOLOGY: In a superstar culture, salespeople tend to use technology individually, primarily to drive up their work volume. A science culture is more collaborative, and prescriptive technology can be used to improve quality, effectiveness and efficiency. It can provide the team with turn-by-turn directions for the next best action with each customer, based on insights gained by others in the organization.

ENABLEMENT: In a superstar culture, it is all about the presenter and the deck - the one great person's presentation. This performance is hard to repeat from customer to customer - even for the salesperson themselves. In a science culture, the team is sharing and documenting what works during each stage of the sales process through dynamic playbooks and blueprints. This doesn't mean scripting, but it does mean granular frameworks and blueprints.

SKILLS: A superstar culture is built on once-a-year training, delivered by those who have not used the taught skills in over a decade, let alone updated them. Instead, a science culture relies on continuous improvement, where best practices are instantly shared, enriched with peer feedback and coached to new team members. In a science culture, seventy percent of learning comes from doing and coaching, twenty percent from peer feedback and only ten percent from formal classroom learning.

TEAM: In a superstar culture, the team is recruited, trained, and incentivized through compensation plans to compete with each other. Instead, in a science culture, collaboration rules. Leaders manage a team not only based on results but also on leading indicators, such as effort, knowledge and skill. They are continuously benchmarking and coaching the team not on how an individual can do a better job but rather on how to share best practices and learn from each other.

Most leaders struggle to work scientifically because the demand to hit revenue goals never stops. Sooner or later things will go awry. In most cases, instead of diagnosing the situation based on data and properly designing the right process, the response is to fire and hire. In other words, the salespeople are considered to be the root of the problem. Thus, the sales leader hopes that by hiring new salespeople, they will get better outcomes. This fire-and-hire strategy often exacerbates the problem because systems and process require stability to take root.

In 2000, James Reason, Professor Emeritus of Psychology at the University of Manchester, published a paper, "Human Error, Models and Management". The premise of his work is that humans are fallible and errors are to be expected, even in the best organizations. In this paper, he states, *"To scale one must look at errors as consequences rather than causes, having their origins not so much in the perversity of human nature as in upstream systemic factors. These include processes that give rise to them."*

He then goes on to point out that "Two important features of human error tend to be overlooked; Firstly, it is not uncommon for the best people to make the worst mistakes. Secondly, mistakes are far from being random, mishaps tend to fall into recurrent patterns."

The latter is what most sales organizations experience when it comes down to hitting quota. In a science culture, the first response when targets are missed should not be to fire people but to inspect the process and identify the root-cause.

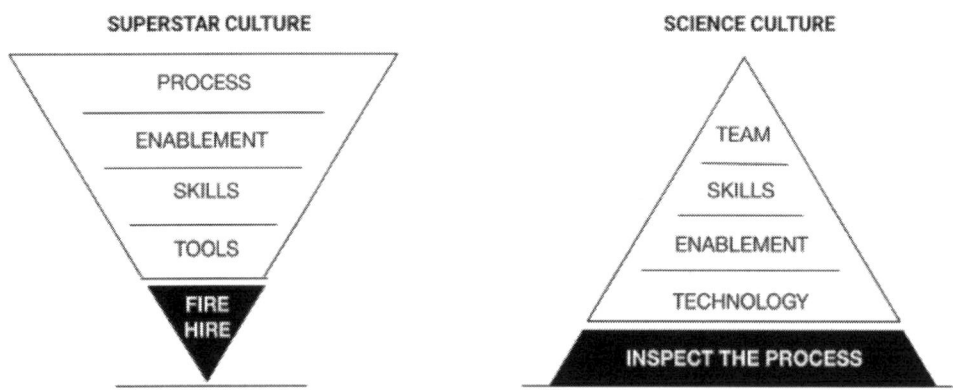

Figure 1.3 When things go awry, inspect the process; don't fire the person

Furthermore, over the past years, organizations have been so ingrained in their thinking that the lack of sales is a people problem; they have focused the use of tools to help fix these issues, not to fix the process. This has resulted in a radical increase in the average amount of tools used by a salesperson with little to no impact on the productivity or forecasting accuracy. The fear is that enablement is headed for the same fate, as it is aimed at fixing a people problem without addressing the underlying process issue.

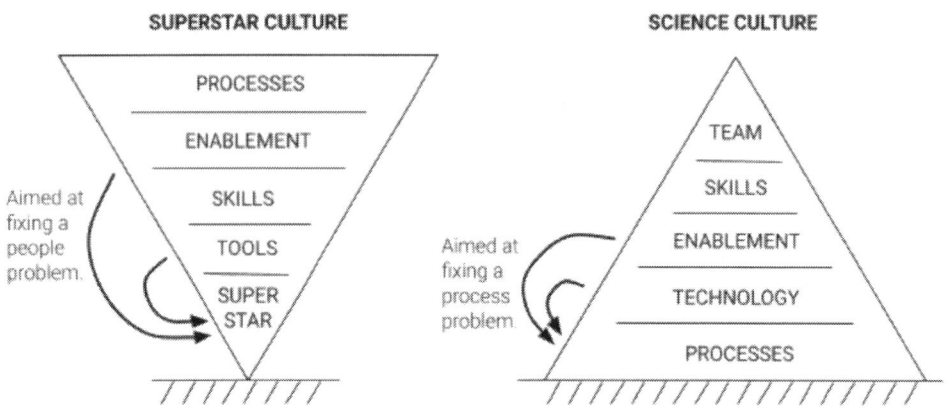

Figure 1.4 Tools and enablement historically have been aimed to fix a people problem

SPECIALIZATION OF LEADERSHIP

At first, we thought that the VP of Sales was responsible for all these elements. Today, it is clear that there are different roles for different people across the sales system. Ask who is responsible for technology and you'll hear Sales Operations! Now ask around who is responsible for the sales process and you'll hear a bunch of titles thrown out, none of which has experience in designing, building or improving a sales process.

We expect that in the years to come, we will see continued specialization of sales leadership roles, with the role of VP of Sales focusing on the realization of growth through the acquisition of logos and/or revenue.

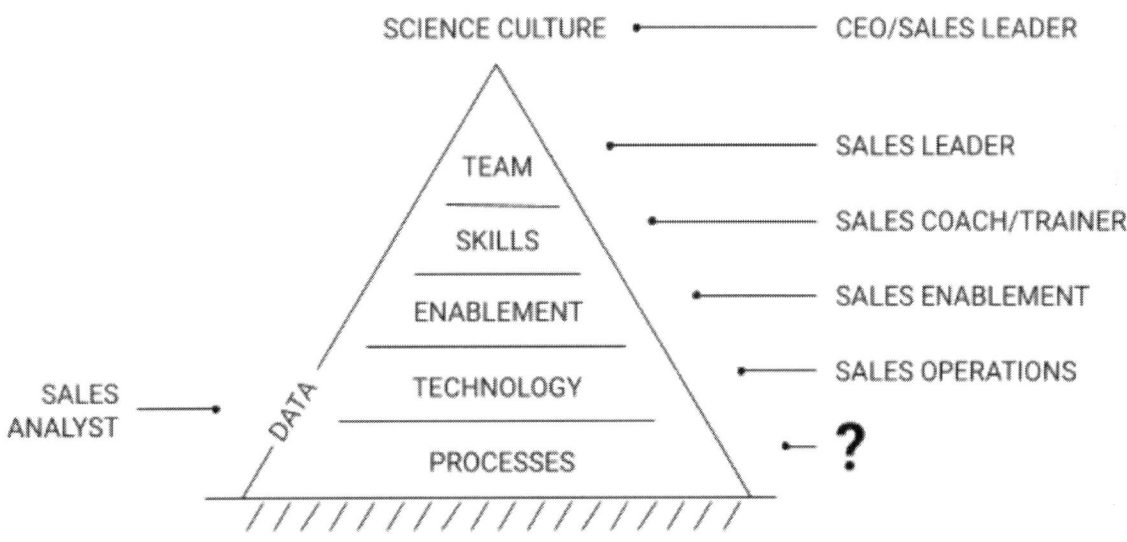

Figure 1.5 Who is responsible for process?

Sales Leader/Organization: Historically, the VP of Sales was responsible for all the functions in the revenue organization. Today however, the complexity of high velocity sales focuses the VP on hiring, metrics, culture, and, most urgently, on logo acquisition. Currently, the VP of Customer Success is responsible for churn and revenue expansion of existing customers. Both report into the Chief Revenue Officer. The VP Sales traditional role is now spread across several others.

Sales Coaching: Organizations large and small are realizing their dependence on younger teams whose members lack the expertise to be productive. There is little time to accumulate this expertise and there is an immediate need for skills training; getting the team the required knowledge in six months that would otherwise take a decade. Whereas many companies still rely on outside trainers, companies are increasingly investing in an in-house **sales academy** to onboard new hires and coach existing teams.

Sales Enablement: The role of sales enablement is to provide salespeople with what they need to successfully engage a client. Traditionally, this was technology and content but we rarely see a single person capable of doing both. More and more, the enablement role focuses on just delivering content to the team.

Sales Operations/Technology: Traditionally, sales ops was focused on keeping up the customer relationship management and marketing automation systems and handling the deal desk. But modern sales organizations use over fifty tools and the scope of sales operations is expanding rapidly. In some organizations, sales operations is referred to as *Revenue Operations* to emphasize the focus on both new logo and existing customer sales. In other organizations, sales operations professionals are adding *Sales Strategy* to their job title to emphasize a focus on sales process.

New roles are emerging and focusing on (elements of) the sales process:

Sales Analyst/Scientist: With the amount of data now available and the valuable intelligence it provides, a new role has emerged: *Sales Analyst*. This role is responsible for the collection and analysis of sales data. They do this in order to increase sales productivity, but they also play a critical role in improving customer satisfaction. They analyze everything from quantitative data to sales funnel flows to future needs forecasts. The rise of this role comes from specialization in sales operations.

Sales Strategist: Some organizations hire a dedicated sales strategist to design, analyze, and optimize the revenue engine. A sales strategist, in this case, often is a "chief of staff" to the chief revenue officer. Sales strategists instrument the sales process and sales team, use benchmark data, dig deep for the root cause of any gaps, and then work cross-functionally to implement processes, coaching, organizational design, compensation plans, and sales technologies to drive growth. The best sales strategists focus on just one key performance indicator each quarter, for example, the sales cycle, the win rate or the deal size. Some organizations also refer to this role as **Business Process Optimization**. A job description of this new role we have been using can be found in the appendix of this book.

TRANSITIONING TO A SCIENCE CULTURE

The change from a superstar culture to a science culture does not come naturally. The good news is that sales is not the first function to undergo the transition. We can look around us and see how others have tackled the problem:

Production Manufacturing uses an approach called Six Sigma, a set of techniques and tools for *process* improvement. It uses a *data-driven* approach for eliminating defects in a process.

Sports Professional baseball uses Sabermetrics to measure and improve performance-driven **functions**. Bill James, one of its pioneers, believed that people misunderstood how the game of baseball was played, claiming that it is actually defined by the *conditions under which the sport is played*.

Development Software development employs Agile Programming, an approach under which solutions evolve through the *collaborative* effort of cross-functional teams. It advocates adaptive planning, rapid evolutionary development, continual improvement, and a flexible response to change.

We have found these varied implementations of scientific rigor have four elements in common:

Element 1. The use of *process* to allow iterative improvement over a short time

Element 2. *Data-driven* decisions in which measurability creates accountability

Element 3. *Team performance* over individual performance creates scalability

Element 4. The use of a common *methodology* creates repeatability

For far too long sales has been perceived as an art practiced by savants. In our experience, there certainly is an art to working with a customer, but it is equal to the amount of art in engineering, or in any other field. If you come away with a single thing from this book, we hope you come away sharing our belief that to scale your sales requires a cultural change to a more scientific approach instead of making organizational changes that perpetuate relying on superstars.

RECAP CHAPTER 1 | **SCIENCE OVER SUPERSTARS**

Over the past years, organizations have been dogmatic about sales performance being a people problem. In a science culture, the first response when things go awry is to inspect the process and identify the root-cause, not to fire the people executing it.

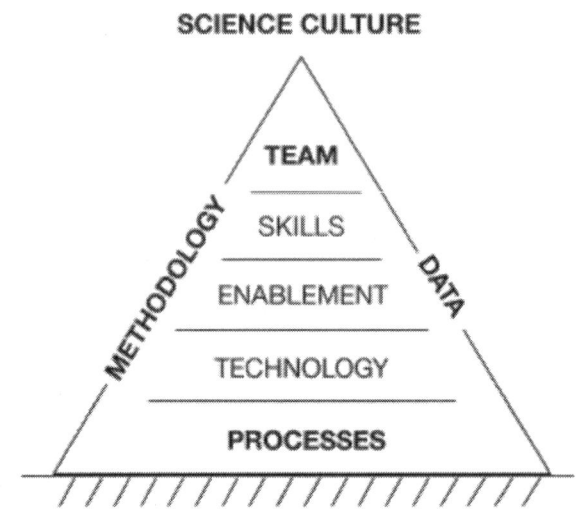

The change to a science culture does not come naturally. There are four elements we have found in other organizations that moved to a more scientific approach:

Element 1. The use of *process* to allow iterative improvement over a short time

Element 2. *Data-driven* decisions in which measurability creates accountability

Element 3. *Team performance* over individual performance creating scalability

Element 4. Use of a common *methodology* creates repeatability

Next, we are going to share some of the changes that are the result of using SaaS as a business model. Before we look forward, we believe it is important to first look backward and understand what got us here in the first place.

CHAPTER 2
CHANGES IN B2B SALES

To explain the changes B2B selling has gone through over the years, you need to understand some of the fundamentals of pricing, in particular, recurring pricing and the impact of the land and expand model. To help understand this, we developed what we call "the SaaS-o-Meter," (Figure 2.1). In the SaaS-o-Meter, we show how businesses operate along an arc between two extremes. On the far left, the buyer pays upfront, as would be the case with internet routers, servers and perpetual software licenses. On the far right, we live in a "no cure-no pay" world where clients only pay for results, such as in online advertising.

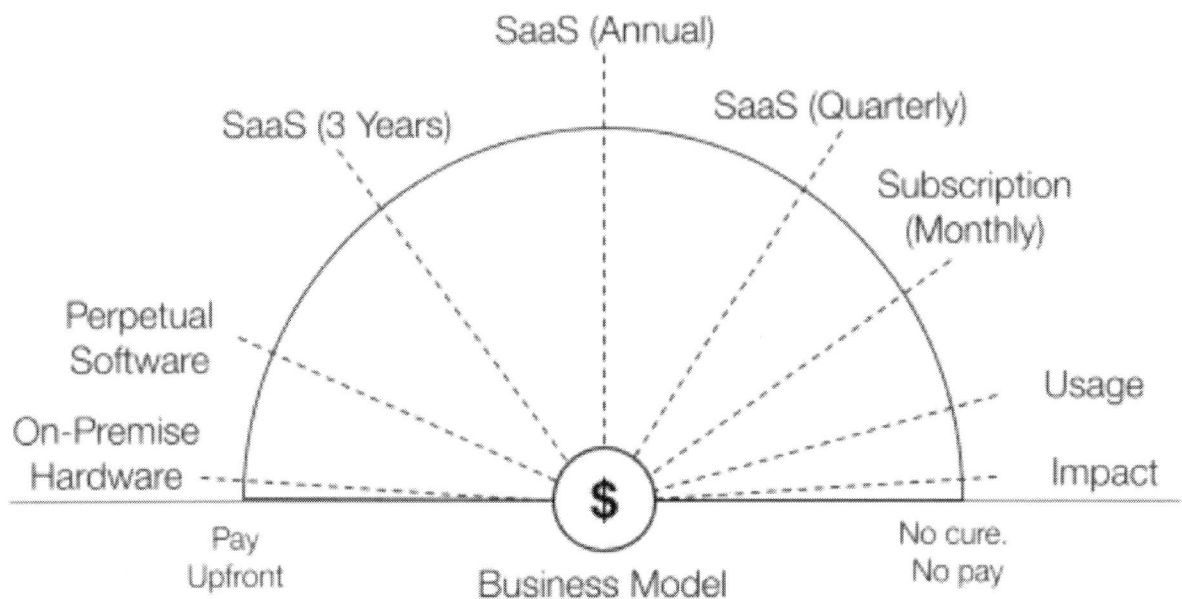

Figure 2.1 Using the SaaS-O-Meter to visualize pricing models

In the middle sits a representative Software as a Service business with a one-year contract paid upfront. To the left of the middle is the three-year SaaS contract which is commonly found in government contracts and security products. Further to the right, we see pure monthly and subscription-based products that evolve into various forms of usage-based pricing.

Businesses can move from left to right as well as from right to left on the SaaS-o-Meter. Doing so not only changes how they price, but how they have to sell!

A Sales as a Science approach means being aware of the impact of those changes, and the impact they have on where a company's revenue operation sits.

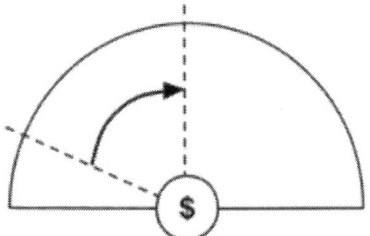
RECURRING REVENUE
One of the common trends is for existing enterprise sellers to change the pricing model to a SaaS model often aimed at capturing the SMB market.

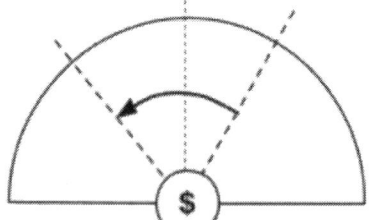
LONGER-TERM CONTRACTS
Existing SaaS companies that sell platform software move to multi-year contracts with enterprises as client acquisition and retention fees take longer to recoup.

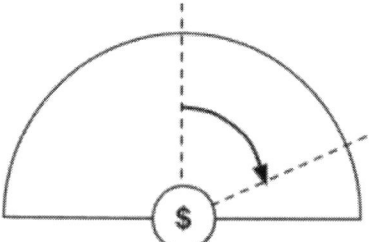
ACCELERATE ADOPTION
Companies move to usage or even an impact-based models to accelerate their growth at the cost of profit. Not every solution is suited to this.

Figure 2.2 Businesses are moving both towards and away from a SaaS model

Let's see how the SaaS-o-Meter works for something like transportation. In the model on the left side of the SaaS-o-Meter, you would buy a car and pay upfront for the promise it holds of getting you to work every day. That upfront payment would not take into account fuel, insurance, parking and other ancillary costs.

Leasing a car is the equivalent of a one- to three-year SaaS contract with monthly payments, in which you still have to pay for the fuel and insurance, but instead of the upfront payment, you opt for monthly payments. Going further to the right, you find daily car ride services, such as Zipcar, and all the way to the right you would find rideshare and taxi services in which you only pay for the actual impact - getting you to work.

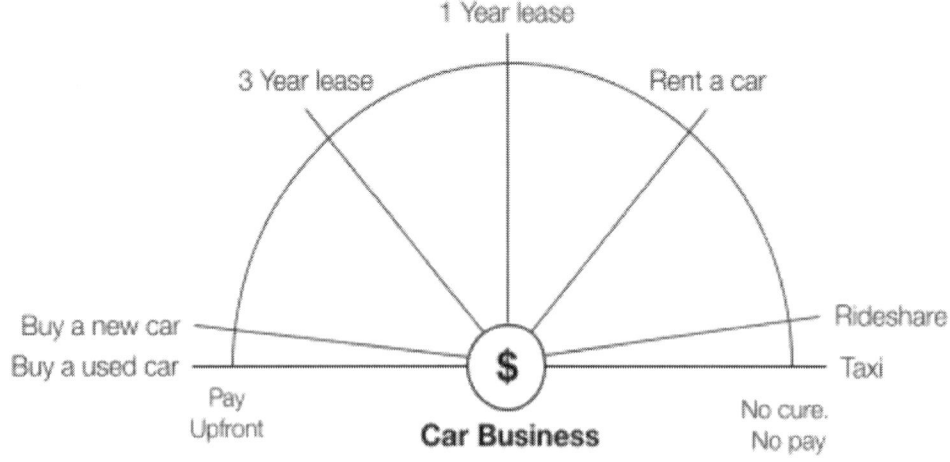

Figure 2.3 Transportation business pricing example

Moving along the arc of the SaaS-o-Meter brings in a series of changes we will discuss next:

Change 1. Power has shifted

Change 2. Win rates have fallen

Change 3. Profits have moved

Change 4. The sales cycle has accelerated

Change 5. The model has become immune to superstars

Change 6. The workforce has become highly specialized

CHANGE 1: POWER HAS SHIFTED

What few, if any, of the sales methodologies in recent years that have accounted for the seismic shift in power between the buyer and the seller is a result of the shift towards recurring revenue and the land and expand business models. It is no longer the case that buyers have to spend a million dollars upfront to buy a perpetual software license for a product which may, or may not, work as advertised. "Usage" has had the effect of converting most software related CAPEX into OPEX. Hence, buyers have much less invested and therefore perceive their risk differently.

On the one hand, it is much easier for customers to sign up for a solution because there is less on the line. On the other, it is just as easy for them to quit. In the recurring model, customers take little risk upfront when they pay as they go. Unless you deliver business impact again and again, customers churn.

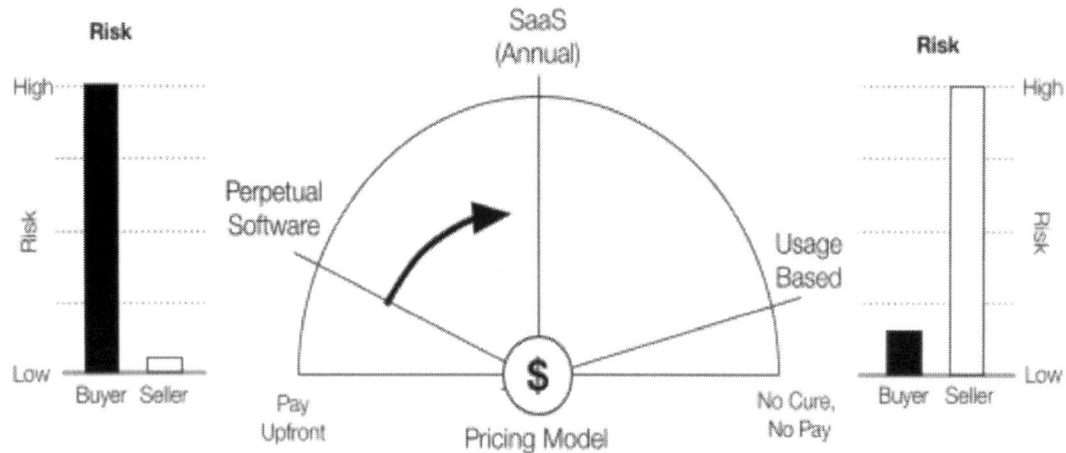

Figure 2.4 Transaction risk has shifted from the buyer to the seller

They don't care what your customer acquisition cost is, or your customer retention cost is, or anything else. All they care about is whether your product has delivered business impact. If you run a SaaS business, you have most likely experienced this shift in risk whereas customers previously would have decided on an enterprise-wide deployment upfront. It is now common to first sample the impact through a smaller pilot before expanding the use of your product to other parts of the organization. This model is often referred to as a "land and expand" model.

CHANGE 2: WIN RATES HAVE FALLEN

In order to make a million dollar purchase, a buyer cannot just go out and submit a request for a quote with a series of vendors. They first need to secure the budget internally. When the project is budgeted, the benchmark on win rate in B2B has historically averaged around one in every three deals. If the win rate of these pay upfront deals fell to, say, one in four, heads would roll.

Today, however, in shorter contracts, we see win rates that vary based on a company's position on the SaaS-o-Meter because companies no longer need a budget to test drive a SaaS solution. The buyer can kick the tires without even a minimal commitment required from the organization. In our experience, shortening the contract duration to monthly lowers the win rate to one in six...or worse.

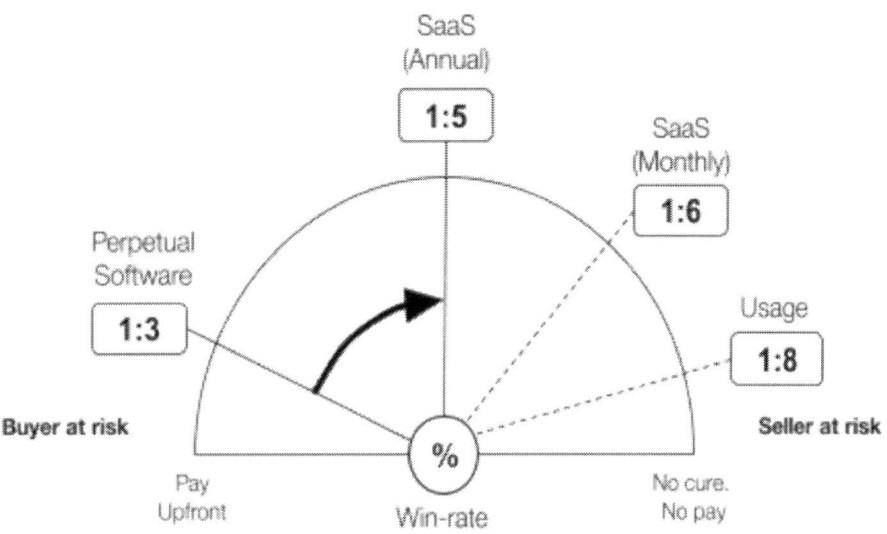

Figure 2.5 The win rate drops as the risk shifts toward the seller

Now you would expect that if you provide part of the service for free and let the client experience the impact, then convert those clients who had a positive impact into a paying contract, the win rate would increase, right? Yet conversion rates in freemium to paid contracts are often lower than one in six. The concept of closing an initial small deal quickly then growing the account is sound, but attention should focus on what you give away for free and for how long. If customers become accustomed to free, they are unlikely to pay you in the future. Also, churn moves in an inverse proportion to contract length as well. Freemium customers churn at the highest rate whereas annual or multi-year contracted customers churn at the lowest rate.

CHANGE 3: PROFITS HAVE MOVED

In 1898, Elias St. Elmo Lewis developed a model that mapped a theoretical customer journey from the moment a brand or product attracted consumer attention to the point of action or purchase. He created a four-stage process; Awareness, Interest, Desire, and Action, or AIDA. This term was made popular when it was famously enacted in a scene by Alec Baldwin in the cult classic movie *Glengarry Glen Ross*. In the AIDA model, revenue and profits are realized shortly after the client signs a contract. Many sales and marketing organizations still are based on a derived version of AIDA in what today is called the funnel.

Figure 2.6 Marketing and Sales Funnel used for perpetual

With the advent of recurring revenue models, the conventional layered funnel as described in Figure 2.6 has become outdated because it views it from the seller's perspective, not the buyer's. To make matters worse, it creates a silo approach in which individual teams focus on their performance at the expense of others in order to hit a target.

A new model is used which is referred to in the industry as a "bowtie." The bowtie must cover two critical gaps; the *impact* stage where sellers must ensure that customers achieve the expected impact; and the critical activity of growing the business together with your customer. These two additional stages create a *system* causing compound growth - in comparison a funnel was designed to achieve linear growth.

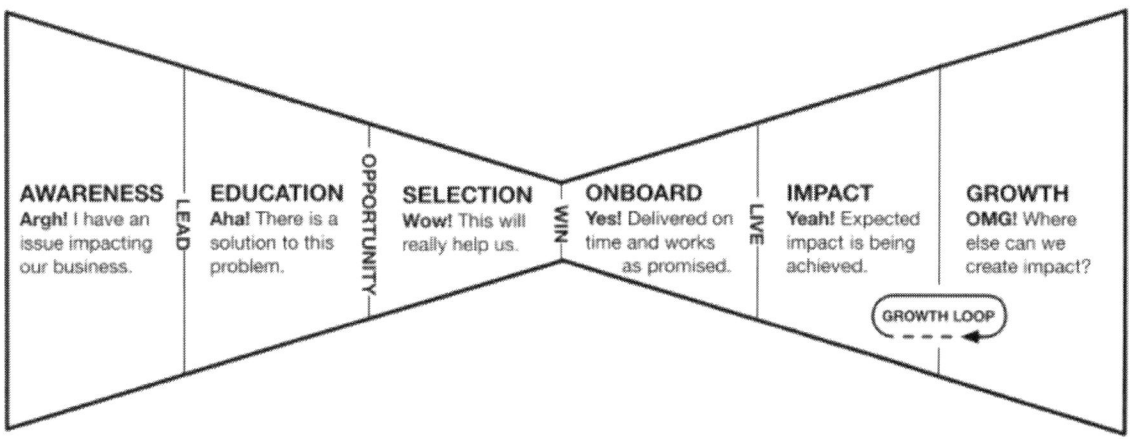

Figure 2.7 The Bowtie based around a customer's experience with two additional critical phases

Using the new bowtie model, we can map revenue distribution and compare the impact of a perpetual model versus a SaaS model with an annual upfront payment.

Table 2.1 Distribution of revenue across three years using a perpetual model

	YEAR 1	YEAR 2	YEAR 3	LTV
Price	$120,000 $120,000			
Upgrade & Support	20% $24,000	$24,000	$24,000	
Annual Contract	$144,000	$24,000	$24,000	$192,000
% of total	74%	13%	13%	

In businesses with a recurring revenue stream, profits are delayed and dependent on future revenues. The table below shows that year-one revenue in a SaaS business only accounts for 29% of the lifetime value (LTV) of a customer. The remaining 71% is based on performance. Can you tell how much additional revenue the growth loop generated?

Table 2.2 Distribution of revenue across three years using a SaaS model (annual upfront)

	YEAR 1	YEAR 2	YEAR 3	LTV
Price	$24,000 $24,000	$24,000	$27,600	
Annual Increase	10%	$2,400	$2,760	
Upsell/Cross Sell	5%	$1,200	$1,380	
Annual Contract	$24,000	$27,600	$31,740	$83,340
% of total	29%	33%	38%	

Some organizations with a recurring revenue model experience this shift in revenue and profits. However, almost all fall short in allocating resources such as people, tools, training, and marketing campaigns to where most of the revenue and profits are generated; the impact and growth stages.

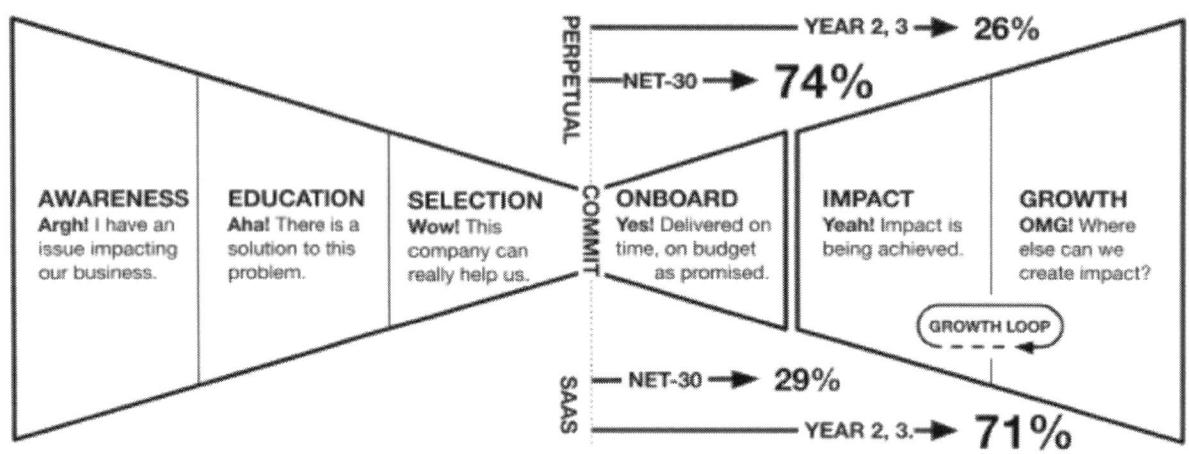

Figure 2.8 Revenue and profits have shifted but resources have not

CHANGE 4: THE SALES CYCLE HAS ACCELERATED

The length of the sales cycle tends to shorten up as we move from a value-based proposal with an upfront payment to impact-based performance. A conventional B2B software sales cycle for a perpetual software license sits between 9 and 18 months. Compare that with the sales cycle of a SaaS contract with an annual contract value of between $12,000 and $48,000, sitting anywhere between 20 to 90 days. Ask attendees of a September SaaS conference, such as Dreamforce, when they need a solution by, and they are likely to say early the following year. Similarly, ask attendees of a perpetual software conference, such as IBC, held in the same month and they'll respond with, "the end of the following year". That is a huge difference in contract values and sales cycles, and therefore in the types of selling resources that can be devoted to each.

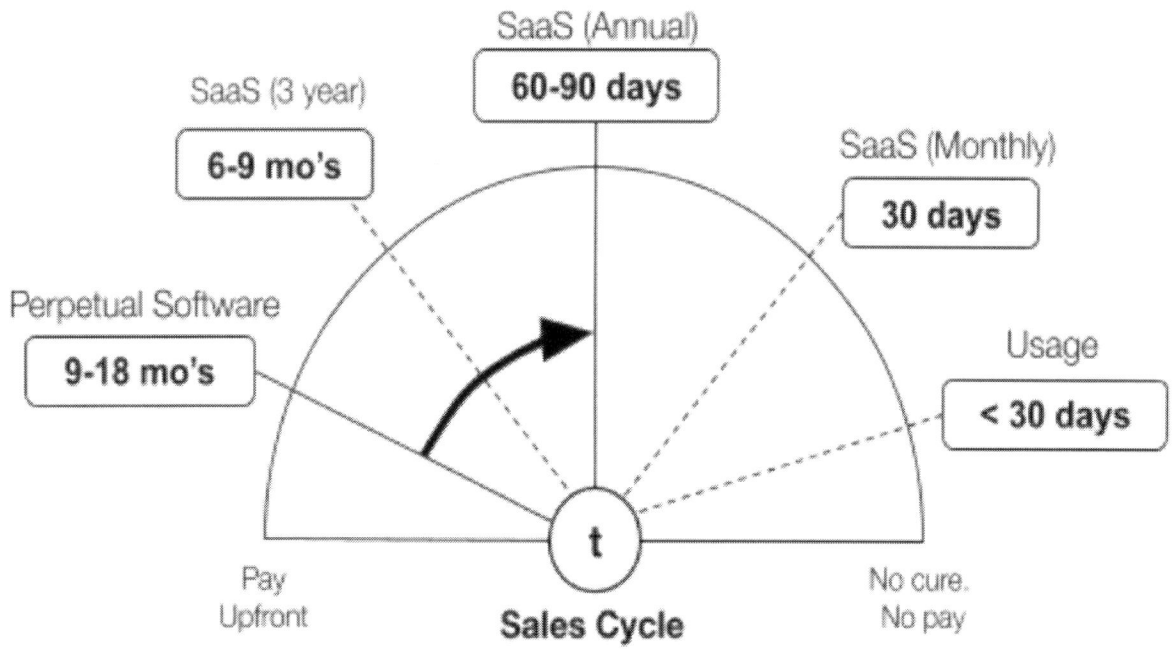

Figure 2.9 The B2B sales cycle has shortened from 9-18 months to 60-90 days

As with anything, increasing speed increases complexity exponentially. Not following up on a request for a demo by the close of business for a SaaS company can mean that the competitor, who intercepted the lead via web chat, has already performed a demo and started the education process while you are still trying to set up a call to diagnose and discuss a demo date. Speed truly matters.

CHANGE 5: THE MODEL HAS BECOME IMMUNE TO SUPERSTARS

Early in 2016 in cooperation with Frank Cespedes of Harvard Business School, we published an article in HBR Magazine under the title: *Hiring Star Salespeople Isn't the Best Way to Grow*. In this article, we described a change away from the Pareto Principle, also known as the 80/20 principle. What we were talking about was the death of the superstar culture that we mentioned in Chapter One. Perpetual license software and on-premise hardware businesses tend to rely on superstars.

Table 2.3 In perpetual software, the top 20% of the sales team attributes 60% of the revenue

Perpetual-Annualized	Bottom 10%	In-Ramp	B-Performers	Superstars
Number of people	1	3	4	2
% of total workforce	10%	30%	40%	20%
Number of deals/year	2	1	2	3
Total deals	2	3	8	6
Average price	$250,000	$250,000	$500,000	$1,500,000
Revenue attribution [$]	$500,000	$750,000	$4,000,000	$9,000,000
Revenue attribution [%]	4%	5%	28%	63%

As you can see in Table 2.3, 63% of the revenue gets attributed to 20% of the workforce. Logically, this means that the remainder 37% of the revenue gets attributed to 80% of the workforce. This impact in the perpetual license model is pronounced not only because superstars win more deals, but more so because their deal sizes are significantly higher.

What we found working with successful recurring revenue businesses is that pricing is standardized thus the deal size is set and only varies based on discount level. As a result, revenue is distributed more evenly across performers on the team. In the next example, which is representative of SaaS businesses, the superstars still close more deals and at a slightly higher price (lower discount) yet they only contribute 34% of the annual revenue.

Table 2.4 In recurring revenue models such as SaaS, the top 20% attributes only 30% of the revenue

SaaS-Annualized	Bottom 10%	In-Ramp	B-Performers	Superstars
Number of people	1	3	4	2
% of total workforce	10%	30%	40%	20%
Number of deals/year	2	1	3	4
Total deals	24	36	144	96
ACV	$12,000	$12,000	$13,500	$14,250
Revenue attribution [$]	$288,000	$432,000	$1,944,000	$1,368,000
Revenue attribution [%]	7%	11%	48%	34%

This means that if we exclude the top 20% of the team, the bulk of your workforce, or the ordinary sales people, SaaS has to outperform their perpetual peers by at least two times. That is a gigantic performance shift and most SaaS sales organizations have not caught up.

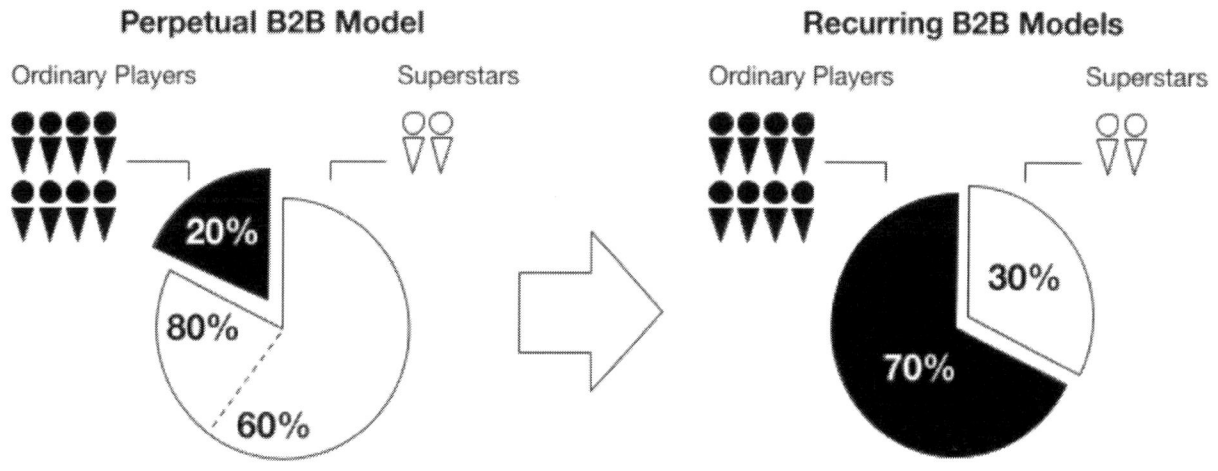

Figure 2.10 The shift to reliance on average performers who contribute up to 70% of goal

CHANGE 6: THE WORKFORCE HAS BECOME HIGHLY SPECIALIZED

The revenue shift to later in the customer lifecycle and the generally lower initial Annual Contract Values (ACVs) have had an impact on the organizational design of companies as well. First of all, with lower ACVs, quotas have come down. For years, the compensation and quota in B2B for perpetual hardware and software sales were around $250,000 in compensation in on-target-earnings for a quota of $4M.

Naturally when sales quotas are lower, the cost of sales in the form of sales salaries has to come down. What has happened is that the market has started to hire less-experienced sales people earlier in their careers. Whereas a traditional B2B software/hardware sales professional was between 35 and 55 years old, today we see entire B2B sales forces at SaaS startups with 25 and 35 years being the average age.

To get less experienced sales people up to speed more quickly and predictably, companies have responded with role specialization. Today it is not uncommon for a sales organization to have split what once was one job for a tenured professional into a variety of roles, including but not limited to:

- Marketing for "Lead Generation" and "Lead Development"
- Market Development Rep (MDR) doing research and responding to inbound leads
- Sales Development Rep (SDR) generating leads via outbound prospecting techniques

- Account Executive (AE) getting initial customer commitment
- Onboarder (ONB) to guide the customer to first value sits with a sales engineer
- Customer Success Manager (CSM) orchestrating the customer's ongoing experience
- Account Manager (AM) helping the customer grow the business

When well executed, job specialization can increase sales velocity and improve effectiveness. Organizations need to ensure that specialization is paired with a well-defined, cross-functional process and job training for each role. Without a well-defined process, customers and win rates will suffer from poor handoffs between functions. We have seen it again and again: Without a well-defined onboarding and coaching program, the reps will fail.

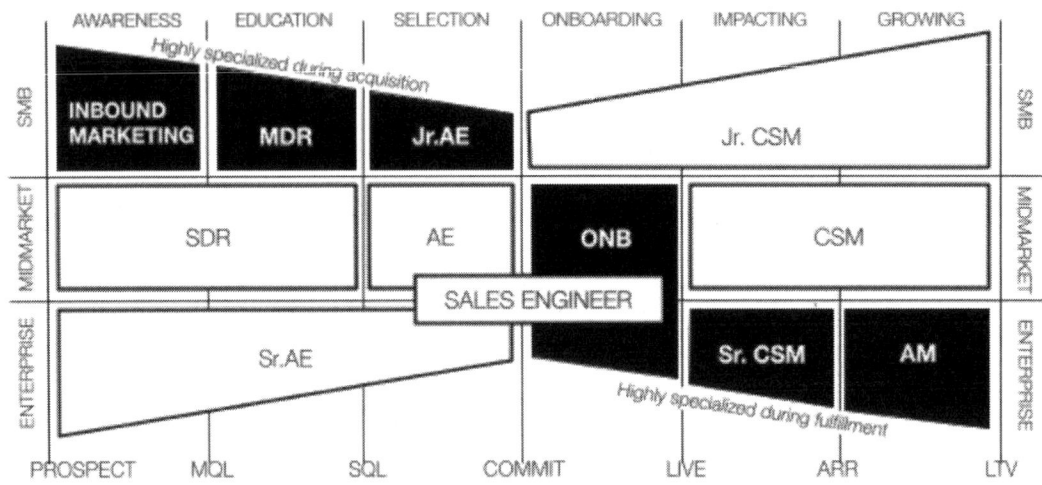

Figure 2.11 *Specialization of roles both by function and market segmentation*

In the figure above, you will notice a shift of specialization; whereas the acquisition of SMB clients benefits from highly specialized roles compared to enterprise clients who benefit from highly specialized fulfillment.

This may run contrary to what one would expect. However, it is common practice for large enterprise deals to be prospected by the most senior, skilled person on the team, not the least. These experienced sales reps use existing clients and personal connections built over a lifelong career to prospect. This explains why enterprise reps expect a premium and flawless service experience by the company for *their* customers, since *their* livelihood and career are at stake.

The specialization of the workforce is not unique to recurring revenue and subscription businesses. Many B2B organizations selling hardware and/or perpetual software have long had a highly specialized workforce, down to a small group of experts doing nothing but preparing quality responses to Requests For Quotations (RFQs).

When selling perpetual software, specialized roles are used to improve effectiveness of winning six-to-seven figure deals. However, when selling four-to-five figure recurring revenue deals, specialized roles are used to increase efficiency! As you may recall, in SaaS, ordinary sales performers need to outperform their predecessors by at least two times. From the perspective of growth, this causes a number of implications:

Implication 1: Because time and money per deal and per salesperson are decreasing, what every customer-facing person says or does at key moments during the sales cycle matters more than ever.

Implication 2: With revenue being pushed further back into the customer lifecycle, everyone in the organization must sell all the time, which really means they must work to uncover and realize more business impact for the customer all the time.

Implication 3: With the sales team comprising less-experienced staff, a prescriptive system to consistently and reliably onboard and guide your team to execute a proven process has become more important.

Implication 4: As customer-facing functions become more specialized, the organization needs a consistent sales methodology that spans from prospecting through selling to growing customer lifetime value to ensure the customer has a consistent experience.

Implication 5: There is an opportunity to use sales technology and enablement to support the accelerating sales cycle and provide customer-facing personnel with turn-by-turn directions about best practices in each moment of the sales cycle.

RECAP CHAPTER 2 | **CHANGES IN B2B SALES**

Changing the pricing model from a perpetual license to a recurring revenue stream results in big changes for B2B companies.

Change 1   The risk of a purchase has shifted from the buyer to the seller

Change 2   Win rates have fallen from one in every three deals to one in every five deals

Change 3   Profits for SaaS are delayed, with profitability as much as 24 months out

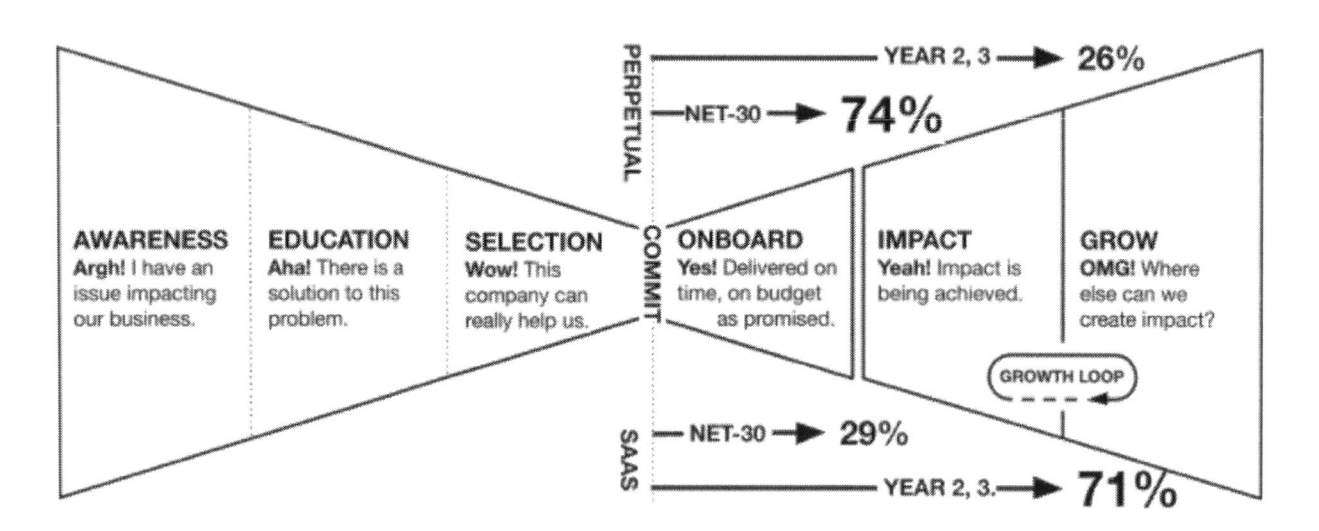

Change 4   Sales cycles have accelerated from 9-18 months to as low as 30-90 days

Change 5   Shift to reliance on average performers who now contribute up to 70% of goal

Change 6   Functions become specialized, increasing the need to use proven processes

To secure recurring revenue requires a group of average performers to work as a team along a uniform approach. Next, we will introduce you to the SaaS Sales Method; a *comprehensive* method for working with customers across all parts of the organization.

CHAPTER 3
THE SAAS SALES METHODOLOGY

Ask the members of your favorite marketing, sales and customer success teams what methodology they use. What answer do you get? Most have none, a few can name one. An answer we *never* get is that people across departments say they are using the same methodology. A methodology describes a defined set of rules, activities, and deliverables that typically serve to solve a specific problem, in this case, to serve the customer. Wouldn't it make sense if all those departments who serve the same customer operate from the same methodology?

Working with marketing, sales and customer success departments across hundreds of companies, we realized that although many things have changed in recent years, organizations have not responded with a *comprehensive* new methodology for working with customers across all parts of the organization. In this chapter, we present the SaaS Sales Method. But let's not rush into that; let's first start with explaining the most common sales methods used today, and the context in which they came into being:

Method 1. Transactional selling

Method 2. Solution selling

Method 3. Consultative selling

Method 4. Provocative selling method

Method 5. Inside selling

And finally

Method 6. The SaaS Sales Method

It's important to note that the discussed methodologies can build on each other and do not have to be mutually exclusive. In fact, today's organizations are required to incorporate many of the key elements from each and apply them throughout their business.

METHOD 1: TRANSACTIONAL SELLING

In a transactional sale, the prospective customer experiences the entire journey through awareness, education and selection in a self-supported way. The client has come to understand the problem they are trying to solve, has looked at a variety of solutions, and has picked a couple of products they like. At this point, they are just looking to get the lowest cost possible for the exact product they are looking for from a trusted distributor, and most likely, the quickest way possible.

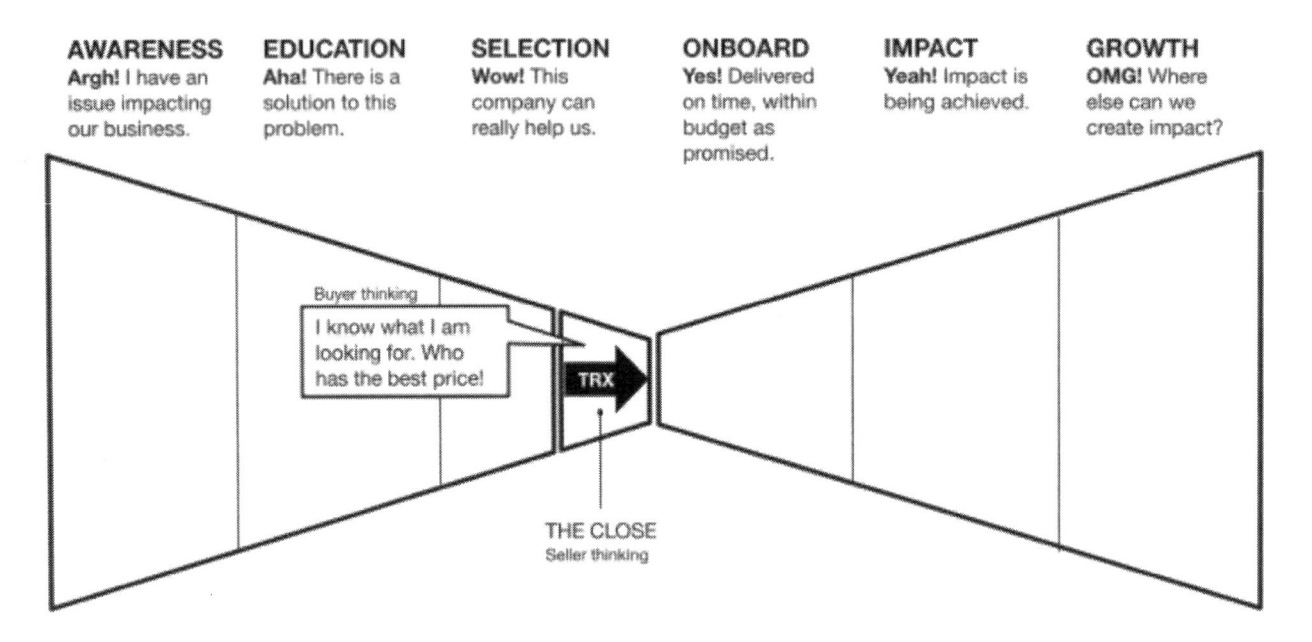

Figure 3.1 Transactional Selling: Focused on closing based on price and availability

Buying a product this way is very mechanical. There is little value to add to the process that a human can do better than a website such as Amazon, which offers price comparison, customer reviews and several shipping options. The frame of reference in a transactional sale is the "close" and the decision criteria for a transactional close are:

- **Price** - Low cost, but does not have to be the lowest cost
- **Maturity** - Must give the buyer confidence that the vendor will provide benchmark level quality
- **Service** - Have a 24/7 support line or online Q&A to address most common questions
- **Response time** - The buyer wants it right away; one click to buy, install and gain impact

If a client needs more help such as determining if the right infrastructure is in place for them to buy then solution selling is the better methodology.

METHOD 2: SOLUTION SELLING

Solution selling is a sales methodology in which, rather than just pitching an existing product's benefits, the seller focuses on learning about the customer's problems and pitches the benefits of the product in that context. It assumes the customer understands their decision criteria and is working to optimize against them. That said, the customer normally needs help understanding whether the product would work in their environment. Questions might include:

- Does it integrate with the customer's existing software stack?
- How to migrate

To answer these and other questions, a customer often prefers to have a meeting, ask a few questions, and participate in a high-level demonstration before requesting a formal quote. Solution selling is closely aligned with inbound lead generation because potential customers often do online research about their problem and find potential vendors who might fit their decision criteria. In a solution sale, the salesperson's goal is to get from demo-to-close as quickly as possible as the customer will continue to shop for a solution. This makes the discovery and demo experiences the most important points in the process. Ideally that means:

- **Diagnosis** - A short discovery of their needs, primarily to justify a demonstration within the context of those needs
- **Prescription** - A quick transition to the demonstration, preferably on the same call, in which the customer gets to see the product working and visualizes how it would impact their business

As sales cycles shorten, we have found that sales organizations often lose deal momentum when their Sales Development Reps (SDRs) become too focused on qualifying the client and setting up a disco/demo meeting for their account executives several days later. In a solution sale, speed matters, and the client is often ready to move ahead immediately. This loss of momentum is amplified when the competitors move to demo right away. Therefore, we recommend that the reps manning a chat channel should be able to perform a demo at the client's request.

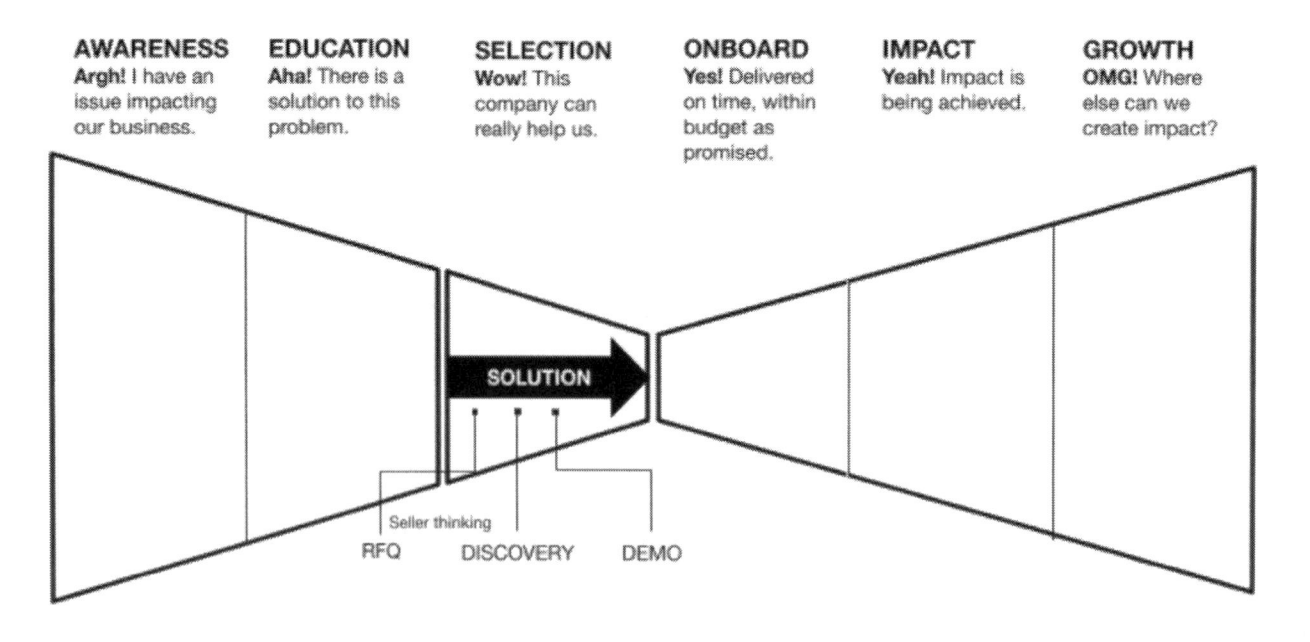

Figure 3.2 Solution Selling: The client knows what they want and need limited additional information

The problem with solution selling is that if you are not on the customer's shortlist based on their decision criteria, you are out of contention without knowing it. Thus, companies wish to avoid this by talking to customers before they determine the decision criteria. This requires consultative selling, a technique necessitating additional skills. We have noticed that though many companies *think* they are selling consultatively, in practice, they are very much still solution selling.

METHOD 3: CONSULTATIVE SELLING

The term 'consultative selling' first appeared in the book *Consultative Selling* (1970) by Mack Hanan. In it, Hanan explores the needs for a selling technique in which the salesperson acts as an expert consultant to the customer. Unlike in solution selling, the salesperson is no longer a talking leaflet. Successful salespeople share valuable industry insights to shape the decision criteria. Instead of waiting for an inbound request, consultative sales people target clients using outbound techniques. The technology that greatly enabled consultative selling was PowerPoint and projectors. This allowed for customization of a client's specific business.

This approach is still the most common B2B sales methodology and can commonly be found when sales teams are large, price points are high, and customers have little information against which to benchmark.

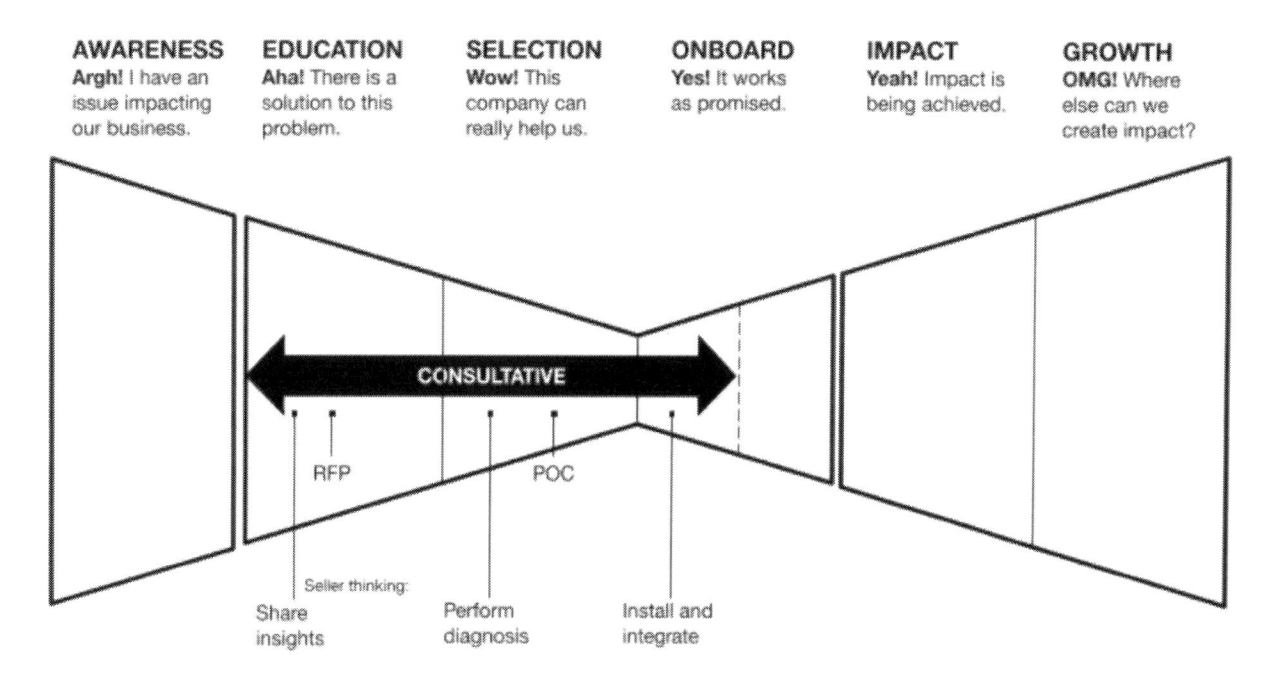

AWARENESS	EDUCATION	SELECTION	ONBOARD	IMPACT	GROWTH
Argh! I have an issue impacting our business.	**Aha!** There is a solution to this problem.	**Wow!** This company can really help us.	**Yes!** It works as promised.	**Yeah!** Impact is being achieved.	**OMG!** Where else can we create impact?

Figure 3.3 Consultative Selling: The client has not yet made up their mind about what kind of solution

In consultative selling, the salesperson is focused on setting the requirements that avoid, or at a minimum, lead to a Request For Quotation (RFQ) with the seller's key strengths in it. The consultative sale extends the sales to a proper installation after the close. The customer is left to use and generate the impact by themselves although sales may return to ask the client to buy more.

The commission structure of a solution salesperson is based on getting the customer to commit to a large and multi-year contract, with the customer generally paying a large part of it upfront. Consultative selling is not a magic bullet, though. Why? It still depends on the customer coming to the conclusion themselves that they have a problem in the first place. What if your solution is so innovative that the client doesn't even understand that yet? In that case, they need Provocative Selling.

METHOD 4: PROVOCATIVE SELLING

In 2009 Philip Lay, Todd Hewlin and Geoffrey Moore shared an article in *HBR* magazine called "In a Downturn, Provoke Your Customer." This article described the best practices they encountered in top-of-the-class salespeople that were able to continue to perform during the downturn. The write-up matched my personal experience after the 2002 Internet bubble burst.

We found that the consultative sales methodology doesn't work when selling innovative solutions because it's based on the client already knowing, understanding and prioritizing the problem *and* solution-based on their view of the impact. *"If I had asked people what they wanted, they would have asked for faster horses,"* said Henry Ford famously. Provocative selling challenges the customer's view of the problem itself, the way to implement a solution, the impact it can have on their business, and even its urgency.

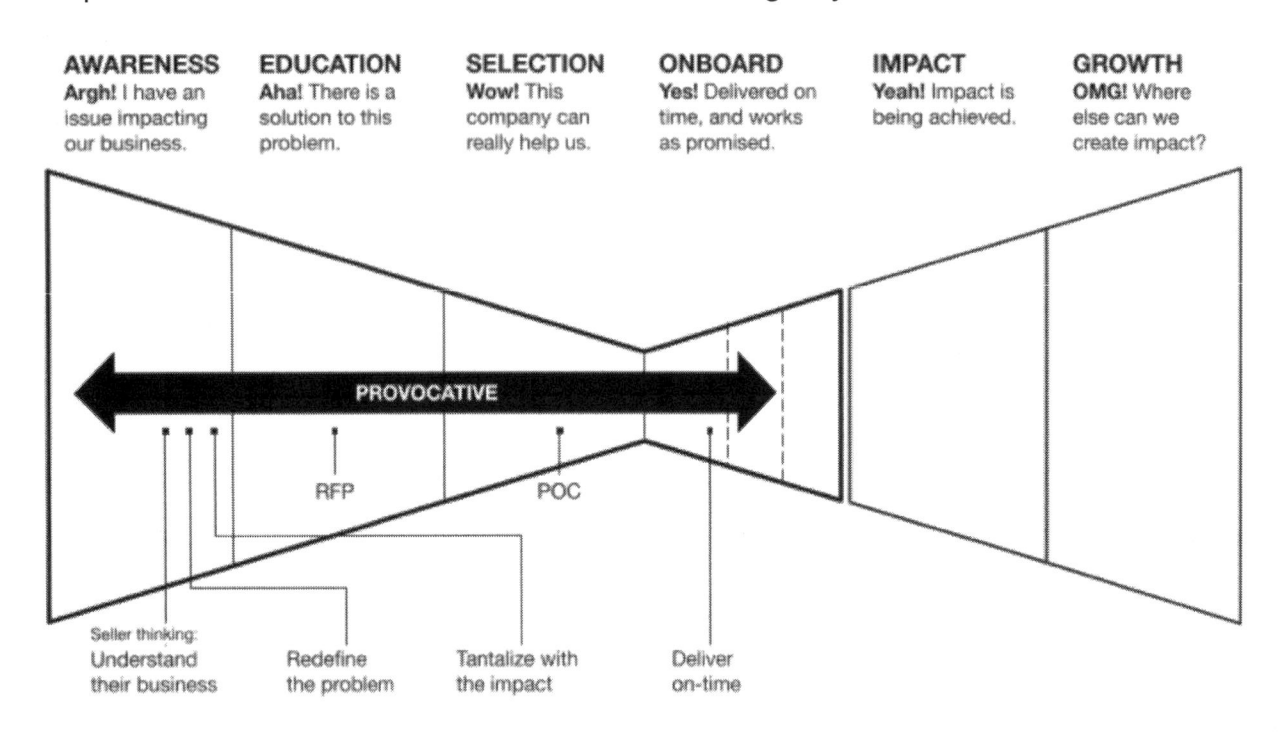

Figure 3.4 Provocative Selling: Challenge the customer's understanding of the real issues

But in order to be effective in provocative selling, you need to understand the market, the problems the market experiences, the solutions needed to solve them, and the impact of the solutions on the business. This means that you need to know your customers' business better than they do. If you provoke a customer based on the wrong information, it will destroy credibility, the opportunity to make a sale - and when performed by a top executive - it can even destroy the reputation of your company.

In the past, acquiring the insights needed to provoke a customer required the sales professional to be an industry insider with 10-20 years of tenure. In contrast, today a sales professional can benefit from an extensive amount of information about the companies and the people they are targeting by performing research online. When done properly, this allows them to become experts in a short timeframe and provide real insight as part of the educational process. They know where to look and are willing to put the time and effort into it.

As depicted in Figure 3.4, provocative selling requires the salesperson to get involved at the very beginning of awareness, helping the customer understand their business in a new way. Their goal is to challenge the customer's view of their own business as a way of introducing the innovation in their product.

METHOD 5: INSIDE SALES

Starting around 2008, a variant of the previous sales methodologies found its way into the marketplace. During the great recession, as financial markets worldwide collapsed, so did the budgets of enterprises that purchased IT equipment, CRM, and ERP software. Up until that point, most enterprises were buying hardware on a five- to seven-year capitalization and software on a three- to five-year capitalization budget or CAPEX. CAPEX is short for capital expenditure, the cost of developing or providing non-consumable parts for the product or system. Its counterpart is operational expenditure or OPEX. OPEX is used for the ongoing cost of running a product, business, or system. As the markets collapsed, the CAPEX budgets melted away. Right at this time, Software as a Service (SaaS) offered a solution on a SaaS contract which could be purchased with OPEX budget, which was still available.

In the inside sales model, prospects, often senior decision makers, are provoked with a very simple, intriguing sales pitch, one that requires minimal skills: *"Do you want to continue to spend a million dollars upfront, or can I interest you in looking at a similar solution for just $5,000 per month."* This provocation is so simple that it can be delivered by marketing through mass cold outbound email campaigns. At the same time, email tracking allowed us to not only learn what prospects responded to but also which prospects engaged and therefore were most susceptible to a cold call.

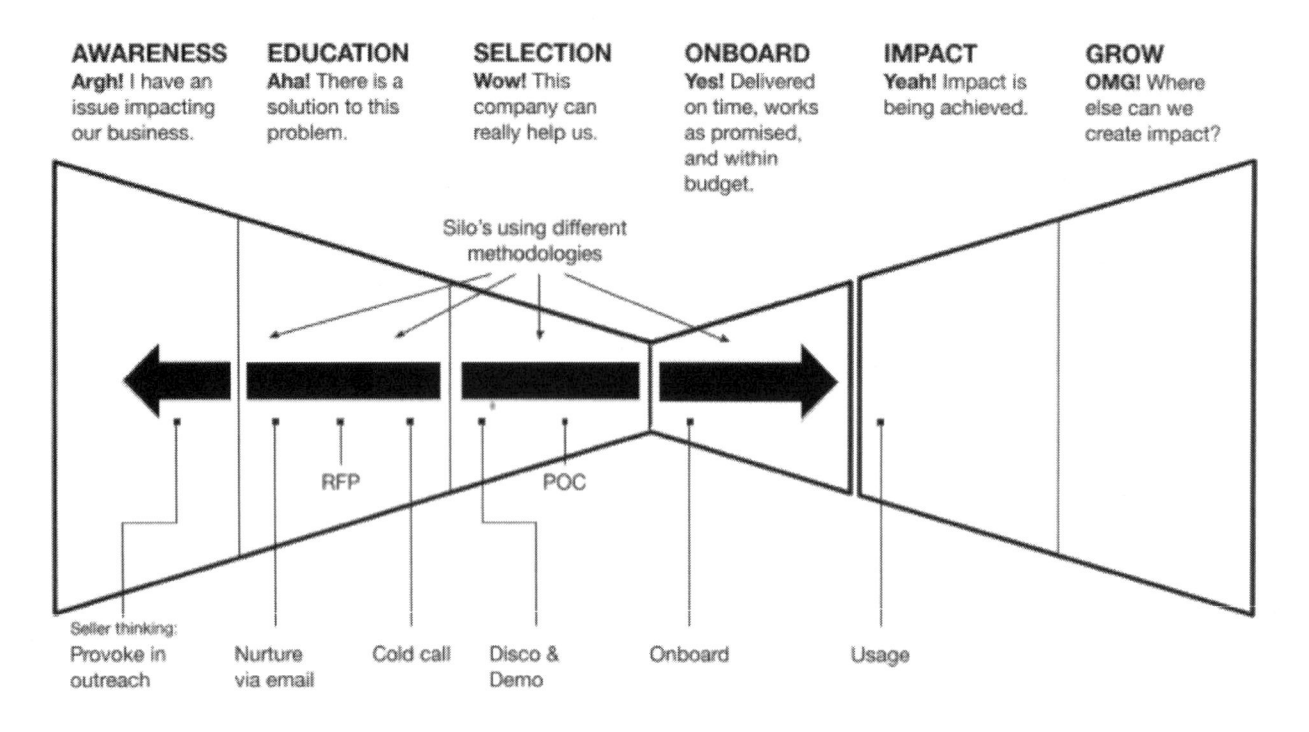

Figure 3.5 Provocative Selling: Challenge the customer's understanding of the real issues

The first generation of Software as a Service products prior to 2008 entered markets in which the buyer and the decision maker were the same person: the Very Small Business (VSB) market. Starting in 2008, SaaS began to filter into the SMB market; in 2012, the mid-market and over subsequent years, it gained foothold in the enterprise market.

But in recent years, many inside sales organizations using the inside sales methodology have found it no longer to be effective or efficient. One of the indicators of effectiveness is the number of sales qualified leads (SQLs) generated per inside sales rep. At 20+ SQLs per month per rep, this model works well. The effectiveness is based on a number of factors such as average sales price, win rate, salaries and so on. However, in recent years, the number of SQLs generated per rep has declined considerably. It is not uncommon to hear less than 10 SQLs per month per rep.

Table 3.1 Some of the lessons learned from inside sales

WHAT WORKED WELL	WHAT DID NOT WORK
✔ Provocative prospecting	✘ Disparate methodology across functions
✔ Use of specialized roles	✘ Volume-based cold outbound
✔ Data driven decisions	✘ Low-cost, unskilled people in critical roles
✔ Use of online selling	✘ Use of the consultative sales method
✔ Content as outbound call	✘ Customer success to grow business from existing clients
✔ Customer onboarding	

Sales leaders unfamiliar with the science that underpins recurring revenue businesses assumed that their drop in SQLs/rep were the result of people problems, and they predictably responded by hiring more people and investing in more productivity tools. Some even relocated their entire inside sales teams to areas with lower wages, such as Phoenix and Salt Lake City.

Inside sales has several elements that worked well and many that today are falling short. In this environment, the goal of a new revenue methodology must not only build on the success of its predecessors but, more importantly, account for its deficiencies.

METHOD 6: THE SAAS SALES METHOD

The SaaS Sales Method is the sales methodology first developed and implemented by software as a service to companies in response to the changes outlined in Chapter Two. It is now finding its way into all business-to-business sales, especially where a large percentage of customer lifetime value is realized after the initial sale. The SaaS Sales Method modernizes and extends prior selling methodologies but does not replace them. It does so by adapting these methodologies to fit smaller initial deals and higher velocity sales cycles where much of the selling happens over the phone or online. The SaaS Sales Method extends selling methodologies to include the processes for demand generation and prospecting as well as post-sales activities including customer success and account management. A hallmark of the SaaS Sales Method is to not only make a customer aware that they have a problem, but to constantly show the impact of the solution in a way that is coordinated and ongoing.

AWARENESS	EDUCATION	SELECTION	ONBOARD	IMPACT	GROWTH
Argh! I have an issue impacting our business.	**Aha!** There is a solution to this problem.	**Wow!** This company can really help us.	**Yes!** Delivered on time, within budget as promised.	**Yeah!** Impact is being achieved.	**OMG!** Where else can we create impact?

THE SAAS SALES METHOD

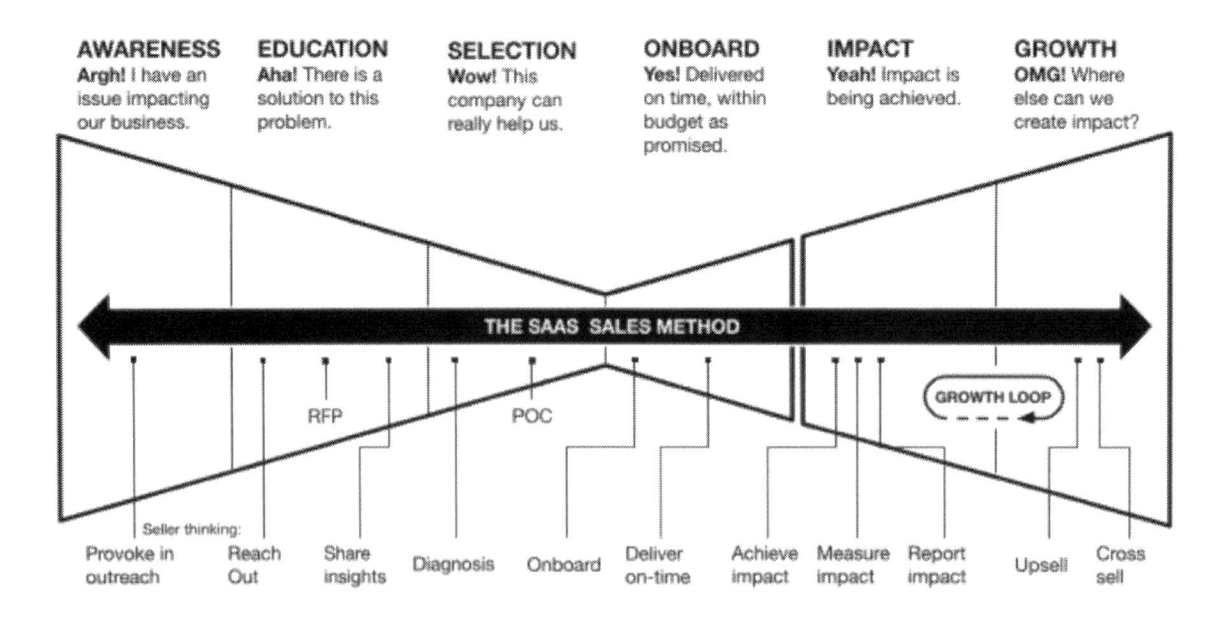

RFP — POC — GROWTH LOOP

Seller thinking: Provoke in outreach | Reach Out | Share insights | Diagnosis | Onboard | Deliver on-time | Achieve impact | Measure impact | Report impact | Upsell | Cross sell

Figure 3.6 The SaaS Sales Method: A customer-centric methodology

This requires that the organization be able to sell using the approach required by the situation - transactional, solution-based, consultative, and/or provocative. It also requires that the customer facing teams on the far left and the far right of bowtie leverage the very same *skills* and *processes* to establish and continue to communicate customer impact. Revenue leaders *must* think about the entire customer journey, a journey in which marketing, sales, and customer success are required to work together as a unified team to tackle the changes of a modern B2B sale. In the SaaS Sales Method, *all* segments of the bowtie should be treated in the same way. A single science culture, go-to-market plan, and sales methodology should apply across the customer journey. Each of the key disciplines should define a clear process, implement it via technology, enable the team, foster key skills, and organize the team in a deliberate and systematic way.

RECAP CHAPTER 3 | THE SAAS SALES METHOD

There are several methodologies that apply in B2B sales, most notably:

Solution selling - Focused on features and benefits

Consultative selling - Focused on value and solving a known problem

Provocative selling - Focused on challenging the status quo and establishing the problem

These methodologies do not specifically service the recurring revenue business model. The SaaS Sales Method offers a new uniform methodology for all customer facing roles in businesses with a recurring revenue model, including but not limited to; marketing, prospecting, selling, customer success, and account management.

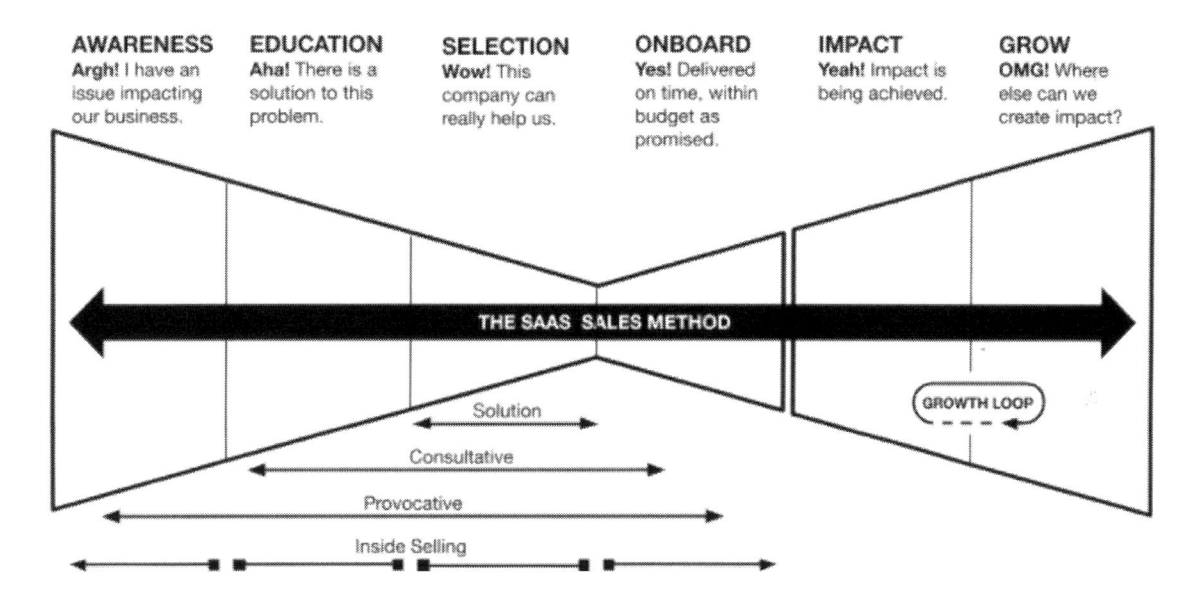

AWARENESS — Argh! I have an issue impacting our business.
EDUCATION — Aha! There is a solution to this problem.
SELECTION — Wow! This company can really help us.
ONBOARD — Yes! Delivered on time, within budget as promised.
IMPACT — Yeah! Impact is being achieved.
GROW — OMG! Where else can we create impact?

THE SAAS SALES METHOD

Solution
Consultative
Provocative
Inside Selling

GROWTH LOOP

For these organizations to work together, they need to speak the common language of data. The next chapter provides a uniform data model and dives deeper into the science behind growth.

CHAPTER 4
THE SCIENCE

Today many organizations are excited about the amount of data that is flowing into their customer relationship management or marketing automation systems. However, with the explosion of data, they often get lost when it comes to how to interpret it. This results in no action or bad action. It is important to measure from the same point and compare it against the same criteria in the same way. Since most decisions in sales today are guided by data, we have to establish the data model. So let's do it. Let's start by standardizing what we are going to measure.

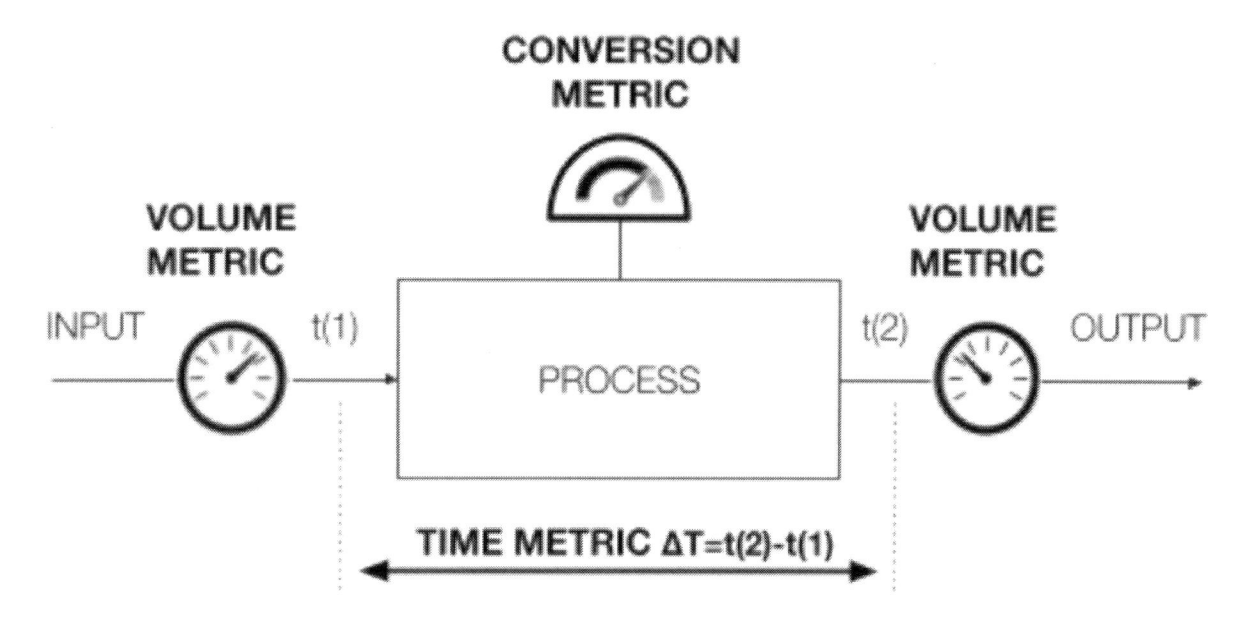

Figure 4.1 A Scientific data model

There are three metrics that contribute to the SaaS Sales Method data model:

Volume metrics measure how many leads, deals, meetings, and wins

Conversion metrics measure how many inputs are needed to generate the desired output

Time metrics measure how long it takes to convert input into output

The most interesting insights don't come from the actual data itself but from the patterns in the data:

Trendline is a comparison of metrics against yourself over time

Benchmark is a comparison to others in the industry using the same model

Performance analysis is a comparison of a person-to-person or product-to-product

Gap analysis is a comparison of metrics against the desired outcome

THE DATA MODEL

Metric 1. Volume Metrics

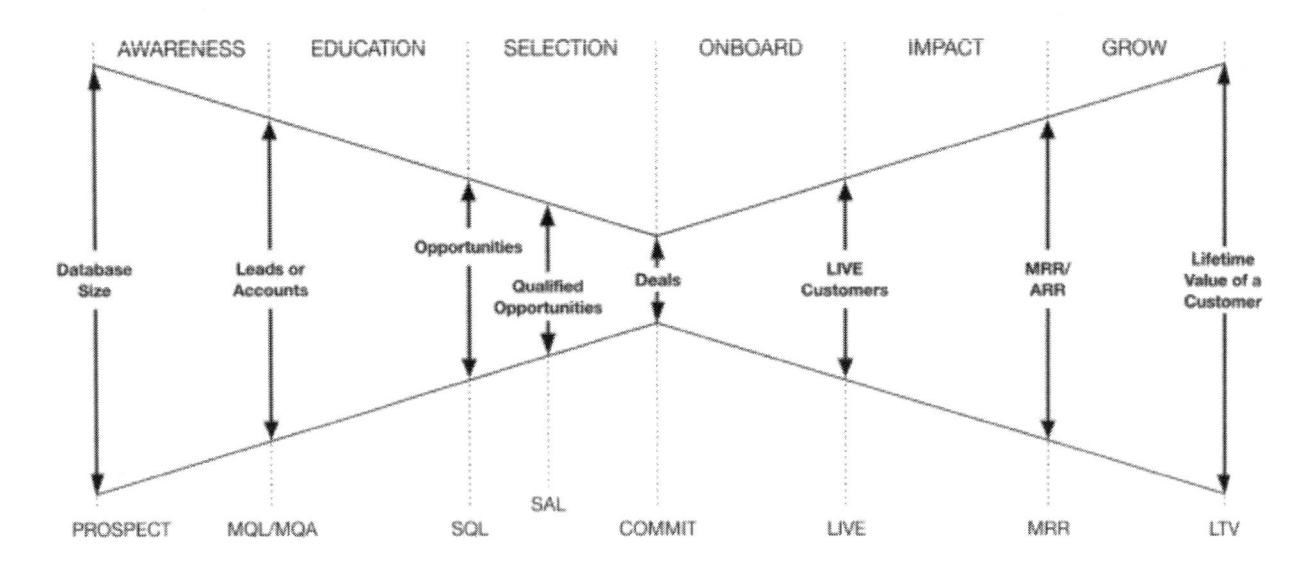

Figure 4.2 Volume metrics measured across the customer journey

Table 4.1 Volume metrics definitions

METRIC	DEFINITION
PROSPECT	A person who expresses interest by visiting a website or other piece of content
MQL	Marketing Qualified Lead, a person who expresses interest and fits the target profile
MQA	Marketing Qualified Account, a company who benefits from the product or service
SQL	Sales Qualified Lead, a person who experiences a pain and wants to take action
SAL	Sales Accepted Lead, verified by the sales team as benefiting from the impact
COMMIT	Mutual commitment to deploy a solution that will achieve impact at a set time
LIVE	Onboarded client, on-time, within budget and the solution can deliver impact
MRR	Solution delivers impact again and again, and a recurring revenue stream is secured
LTV	The revenue an account generates over its lifetime, net of churn and including growth

What comes first, an SQL or SAL?

Do an image search on SQL and FUNNEL and you will notice that most images depict a process where marketing delivers SALs and then sales qualifies them as SQLs. This is the wrong order of operations. In sales, you first qualify then you accept. When sales accepts a lead, it is then held accountable for the win rate and the sales cycle.

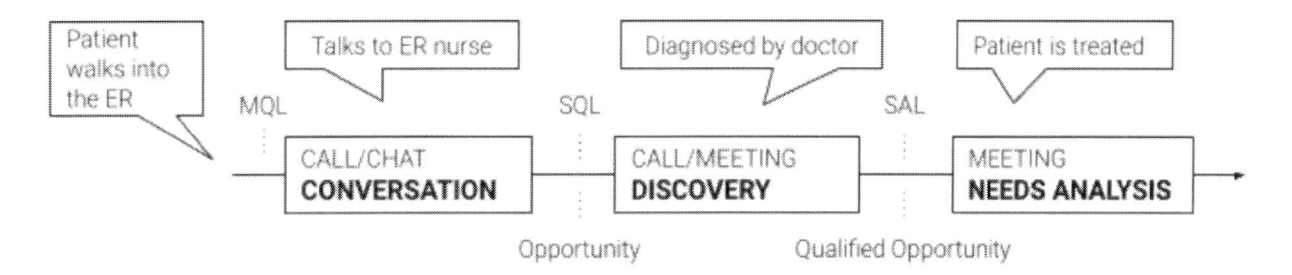

Figure 4.3 First a conversation, then a discovery call to perform a diagnosis, then sales accepts the opportunity

In order to clarify this concept, think of a visit to the emergency room where both the quantity and quality of treatment is based on the diagnosis.

Table 4.2 Example of definition criteria based on volume metrics

CRITERIA	PROS-PECT	MQL	SQL	SAL	WIN	LIVE	MRR	LTV
Is it a fit?	Yes	Yes	Yes	Yes	Yes	Yes	Yes	Yes
Engages with selected content?		Yes	Yes	Yes	Yes	Yes	Yes	Yes

Meets with an expert to discuss impact?			Yes	Yes	Yes	Yes	Yes	Yes
Impact identified and we can solve it				Yes	Yes	Yes	Yes	Yes
Executed mutual commitment					Yes	Yes	Yes	Yes
First impact achieved?						Yes	Yes	Yes
Recurring impact achieved?							Yes	Yes
Total lifetime impact achieved?								Yes

Metric 2. Conversion Metrics

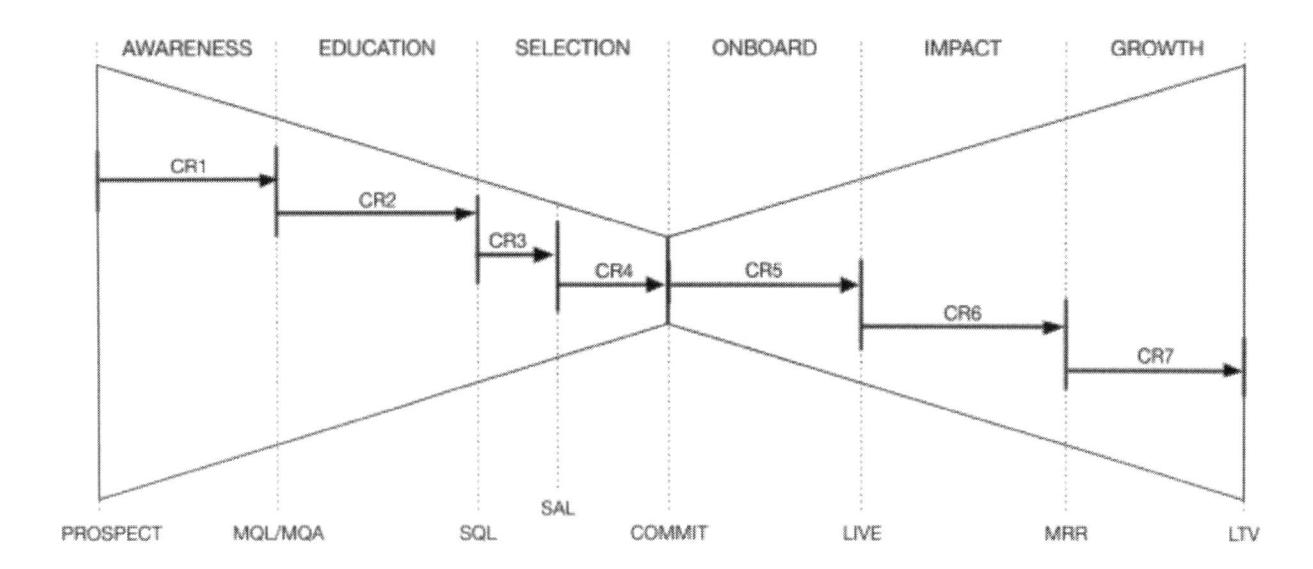

Figure 4.4 Seven conversion metrics

Table 4.3 Conversion metrics definitions

METRIC	REFERENCE	DEFINITION
CR1	PRO→MQL	Prospect to MQL rate, indicative of the quality of the database
CR2	MQL→SQL	MQL to SQL rate, indicative of the quality of lead development campaigns
CR3	SQL→SAL	Showrate, hand-off, indicative of the quality of the prospecting work
CR4	WR	Win rate, indicative of the quality of the sales process and the sales skills
CR5	Onboard Churn	Churn during onboarding, indicative of quality of the client experience
CR6	Usage Churn	Indicative of the stickiness of the service; lack of impact results in churn
CR7	Expansion	Growth of the business during the length of the contract

Importance of SQL to SAL Conversion Metric

When you look at conversion rates, CR3 and CR4 stand out. CR3 refers to how many meetings were set for the sales team versus how many of those turned into an opportunity. CR4 refers to how many opportunities it takes to win a deal, or win-rate. There are several reasons why CR3 is not 100%:

No-shows: Prospects who commit to a meeting simply to get you off the phone during the outbound cold call but never show

Unqualified: Prospects who upon further review, can't benefit from the impact the solution provides at this time

In the case of a two-stage organization, the sales development rep (SDR) had a short conversation with the client who agreed to a discovery call with the sales manager or account executive (AE). We have outlined some of the process and team issues based on the combination of two conversion metrics.

Table 4.4 An example of using Qualification Rate (CR3) and Win Rate (CR4) to evaluate team performance

		CR3: SQL to SAL CONVERSION BY THE SDR			
		<60%	80%	>95%
CR4: WIN RATE BY THE AE	<10%	Process issue! Lots of cold calling with no relevance	Train the AE on diagnosing; Are they working as a team?	Train SDR to qualify and AE to diagnose on *priority*
	20%	Train the SDR on identifying deals that have a pain	Effective and efficient team; Record the process	Add an AE to the SDR; Identify the source of leads!
	>25%	Train the AE to stop taking on just the ready-to-close deals	Add an AE to close more deals	Add a sales team you are in a hot market

Metric 3. Time Metrics

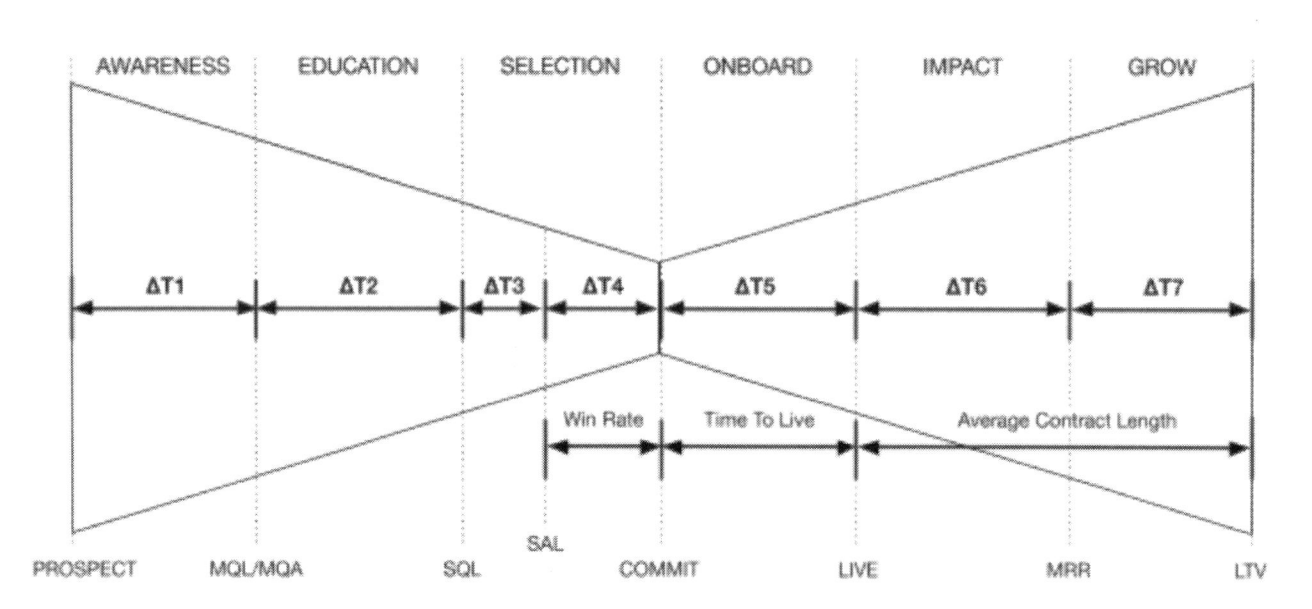

Figure 4.5 The time it takes to convert one metric into another metric

The length of time it takes to convert one metric into another is determined not by the actual activity in the process but by the waiting time in between the processes. For example, it may take five minutes to write an email invite to an event, but it can take days to get a response.

Table 4.5 Time metrics definitions

METRIC	DEFINITION
ΔT1	Duration of prospecting before engagement is achieved, indicative of the quality of content
ΔT2	Duration of the prospecting campaign, indicates the quality of sequences used
ΔT3	Time it takes to set up meetings and convert them into qualified opportunities (ideally <5 days)
ΔT4	Sales cycle indicates the ability of a sales manager to navigate through the client's process
ΔT5	Time to live indicates the complexity of a product, anywhere from seconds to weeks
ΔT6	Time until a client achieves the desired impact, often 6-18 months
ΔT7	Time to achieve penetration of an account, often measured in years

Benchmarks

To give you a point of reference to compare against, below are key metric examples that vary based on Annual Contract Value. Note these will differ by market, region, and vertical.

Table 4.6 Key metrics as a function of the Annual Contract Value

ACV	CR1	CR2	CR3	CR4	T4	CR5	CR6	CR7
<$1k	5%	15%	80%	15%	1-10	95%	90%	5%
$1k-$5k	10%	20%	85%	17%	10-20	96%	92%	6%
$5k-$25k	15%	20%	90%	20%	30-60	97%	95%	7%
$25k-$50k	20%	25%	95%	22%	60-90	99%	96%	10%
$50k-$1M	30%	25%	100%	28%	90-180	95%	97%	15%

When a fast response backfires...

We've all been there...you finally found what you wanted but you can't get it until you *"talk to someone."* You leave your phone number, enter your email address and wait for someone to contact you. How long will you wait, or how often will you check your inbox? Doing some research shows that people tend to wait at most a few minutes, after that they are off to a competitor. Clearly time is of the essence!

This may explain why one of the most common marketing mishaps involves an inbound lead or MQL. When a client reaches out, they generally have a pain that motivated them to do so. As a seller in that first conversation, we like to make sure they are a fit before we schedule a discovery/demo call. As we just discussed, an inbound call is time sensitive: The faster the response, the higher the chance of a successful outcome. In general, an inbound process comprises a series of actions, for example: place a phone call, leave a voicemail, follow-up with an email. We have found that the process is often rushed for the wrong reasons. Let us explain: A client downloads a research paper on your website and provides their email address. This kind of lead in many cases is miscategorized as an MQL. Thus, the development rep calls immediately, leaves a voicemail and sends a follow-up email, as if the client had expressed a pain. But the client never did express a pain. European clients would feel intimidated by the assertive follow-up.

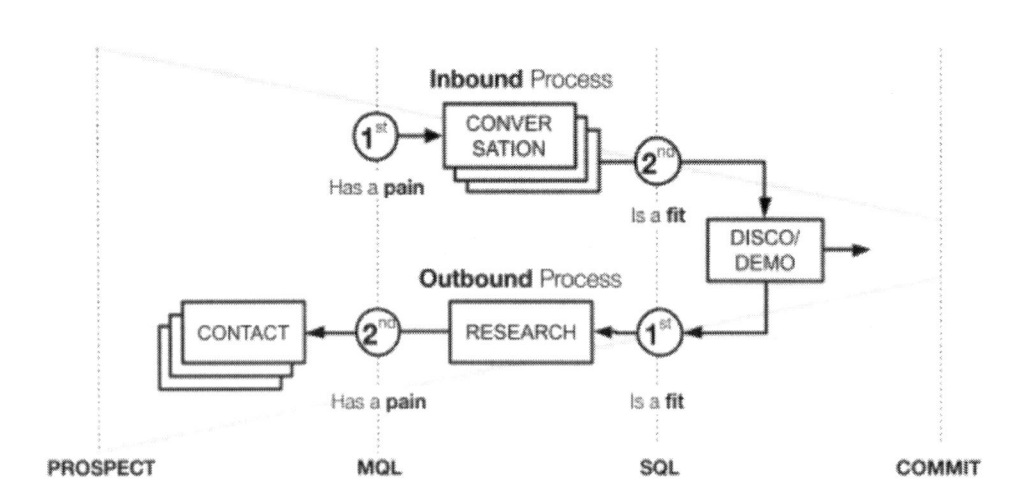

Figure 4.6 Right action sets of the wrong process

Clearly not every MQL is created equal. Instead, this "MQL" should have gone into the outbound process where research should have been performed to determine if this client has a pain.

Table 4.6 Not all inbounds should be treated equally

True Inbound	Quasi-Inbound
• Talk to sales • Schedule a demo • Contact us	• Download of an online asset • Sign-up for a webinar • Visited the pricing page
Being *fast* is most important.	Being *relevant* based on research is more important than being fast.
Next step: Inbound Process	Next step: Outbound Process

THE MATH THAT DRIVES REVENUE GROWTH

As leaders, we have all been in the situation when our sales team is falling short of sales targets. In that circumstance, we - and pretty much everyone we have worked with - tend to respond by thinking about how many more deals we have to add. If we are sophisticated, we also think about how many incremental meetings we need to have, how many more (sales) opportunities, and how many more (marketing) qualified leads we need in order to achieve the goal. We have thought, in other words, in additive terms. This is the result of each department working by itself with an individual additive goal. This approach is the very essence of silo mentality.

However, revenue generation is not a one-time thing that happens in one meeting, performed by a single person. It is rather the product of connected activities across a series of meetings working together in a system. The system is based on connected revenue propulsion systems operating in two distinct stages.

STAGE 1. CUSTOMER ACQUISITION

During customer acquisition, we commonly see different processes at play as in the figure below. Each process is based on a series of interactions and each interaction has a conversion. The end result of the process is the product of the conversion rates (CR).

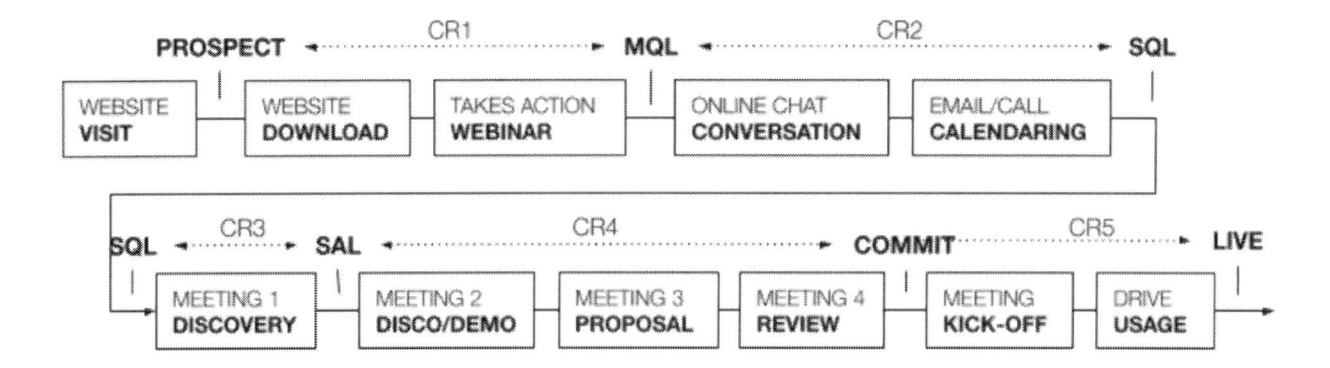

Figure 4.7 Five processes each consisting of a series of basic activities

Based on the above process, we can now calculate the MRR by multiplying one conversion rate with another:

Formula 4.1 Revenue Acquisition

$$MRR_{NEW} = Prospects \cdot CR1_{MQL} \cdot CR2_{SQL} \cdot CR3_{SAL} \cdot CR4_{COMMIT} \cdot CR5_{LIVE} \cdot Price$$

$$MRR_{NEW} = Prospects \cdot \prod_{n=1}^{5} CR(n) \cdot Price$$

Based on this formula, we have come to the realization that revenue is not the sum of deals, but the product of conversion rates creating multiplicative impact. Massive changes in outcomes are therefore possible by making marginal improvements on the performance of single tasks within the system.

For example, a 10% improvement across the seven actions; number of prospects, CR(n), and price, results in nearly 1.95x the revenue. In an additive world, we would have said that to double sales would require twice as many leads, or double the number of salespeople.

STAGE 2. RECURRING REVENUE

We just learned how to double our new recurring revenue stream MRR (new) based on multiplicative growth by improving each conversion rate by 10%.

Even more powerful, the recurring stage gains from compound growth. This is based on a formula used by every financial institution to calculate investment potential. The elements creating compound growth are; the newly acquired revenue from above, the churn (CR6), the upsell (CR7), and the number of periods over which the interval is measured.

Formula 4.2 Compound Impact of Recurring Revenue

$$ARR_{GROWTH} = MRR_{NEW} \cdot (1 + CR6_{churn} + CR7_{upsell})^{number\ of\ periods}$$

This is where we differentiate between a SaaS business with a monthly model vs those who operate on an annual model. A contract based on a monthly service has 12 periods in a year, compared to an annual contract which has only one period. In the annual model, there is no benefit of compound impact as the number of periods is one.

Table 4.7 The compound impact of MRR calculated over a 12-month period

PERIOD	1	2	3	4	5	6	n	12
MRR (new)	$ 10,000	$ 10,000	$ 10,150	$ 10,302	$ 10,457	$ 10,614	..	$ 11,605
CR[6]: -1.5%	$ -	$ (150)	$ (152)	$ (155)	$ (157)	$ (159)	..	$ (174)
CR[7]: +3.0%	$ -	$ 300	$ 305	$ 309	$ 314	$ 318	..	$ 348
MRR (Growth)	$ 10,000	$ 10,150	$ 10,302	$ 10,457	$ 10,614	$ 10,773	..	$ 11,779
	$ 10,000	$ 20,150	$ 30,452	$ 40,909	$ 51,523	$ 62,296	..	$ 130,412

In a *monthly* model, with churn of 1.5% and upsell of 3%, each month the ARR contributed is:

$$ARR_{ANNUAL} = \$10,000 \cdot (1 - 1.5\% + 3.0\%)^{12\ months} = \$130,412$$

In an *annual* model, with churn of 6% and upsell of 10%, each month the ARR contributed is:

$$ARR_{ANNUAL} = \$120,000 \cdot (1 - 6\% + 8\%)^{1\ year} = \$122,400$$

We can now apply the average contract length or ACL to calculate the Lifetime Value (LTV) and compare the increase in annual revenue by extending the contract from 30 to 33 months:

$$LTV = MRR_{NEW} \cdot (1 - CR6_{churn} + CR7_{upsell})^{ACL}$$

$$LTV = \$10,000 \cdot (1 - 1.5\% + 3.0\%)^{30\ months} = \$375,387$$

$$LTV = \$10,000 \cdot (1 - 1.5\% + 3.0\%)^{33\ months} = \$422,986$$

Putting these two stages together, the 10% improvement across the board contributes a whopping 2.37x more in revenue over the lifetime of the customer.

$$LTV(+10\%) = \$19,487 \cdot (1 - 1.35\% + 3.3\%)^{33\ months} = \$890,793$$

RECAP CHAPTER 4 | A SCIENTIFIC MODEL

The SaaS Sales Method is built on the idea that revenue is the product of connected activities across a series of meetings working together in a system. To take advantage of the unique characteristics of a system, companies must measure and optimize around Volume metrics (#), Conversion metrics (CR), and Time metrics (ΔT). This model develops a 2-stage revenue propulsion system:

Stage 1. Customer Acquisition: System impact consisting of a series of small improvements across the board to create an *exponential* one-time impact

Stage 2. Recurring Revenue: A compound impact based on the churn, upsell and contract length metrics

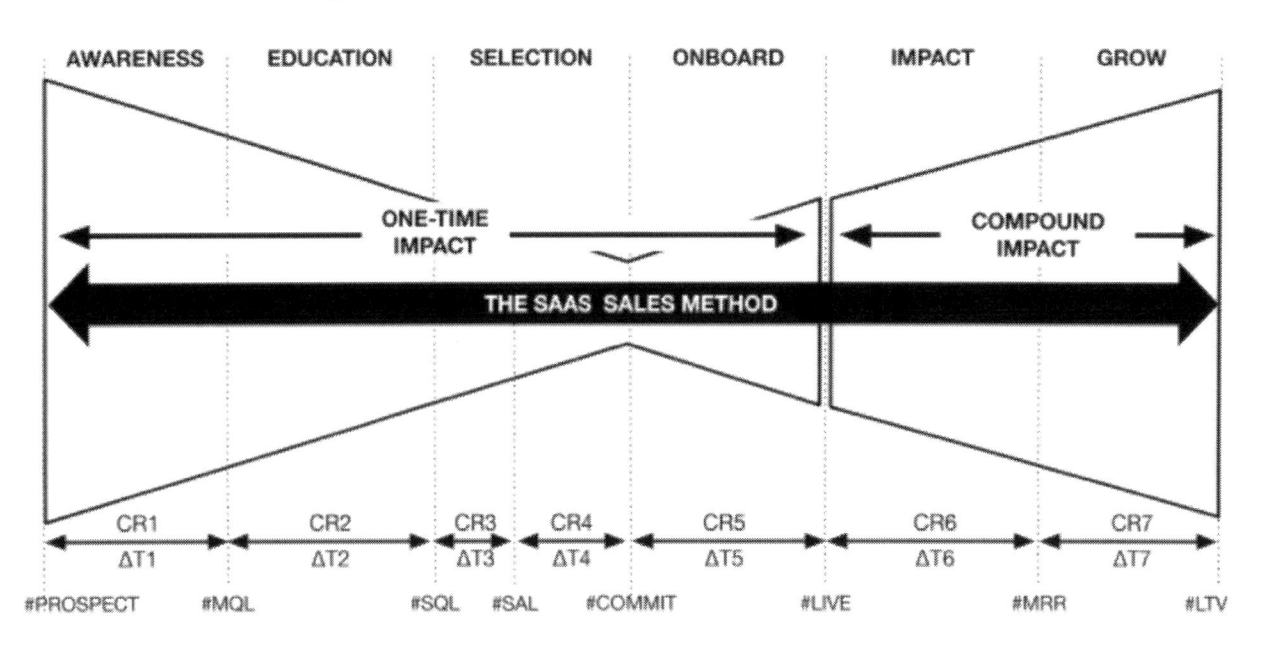

Making a small improvement across a series of actions results in exponential growth and this provides a disproportionate amount of revenue and profit. Next, we are going to identify several key moments that we can use to optimize against.

CHAPTER 5
MOMENTS THAT MATTER

One of the top-rated hotels in Los Angeles is The Magic Castle. People who have visited there walked away with fond memories and give it a 4.8 star rating, higher than many premier hotels. However, if you look at the pictures online, you'll be quick to notice its budget motel-look and feel with the hot tub-sized pool. How can this two-story apartment complex from the 1950s be one of L.A.'s top-rated hotels!?

What makes this hotel unique is the service. Let's just take one of the special moments they have created: *The Popsicle Hotline*. There is a cherry-red phone mounted to a wall near the pool. When you pick it up, someone will answer with "Hello, Popsicle Hotline." You can place an order of popsicles, and moments later, a staffer wearing white gloves delivers your cherry, orange, or grape popsicles poolside. On a silver tray. Complimentary!

You see… what The Magic Castle has figured out is that, to delight customers, you need not obsess over every detail. You just over deliver on a few moments that matter most to the customer. Then customers will forget about the small swimming pool and underwhelming room décor. What we have found is that in sales too, there is a lot of obsession over every interaction with a client, what they downloaded, how many seconds were they on a slide, did they watch the video, did they open the email. There is way too much detail to keep track of!

Instead, we believe that, like The Magic Castle, there are a few special moments that need your attention, and if you get these moments right, they work in concert to give you a great year. These are called the Moments That Matter or MTMs. Everything else can pretty much fall away as long as you get these moments right. And guess what? When you correspond each key moment to a conversion point, we talked about it in the preceding chapters, we have a way to impact growth. This piece of insight, while simple, has a lot of implications.

There are a few fundamentals you must get right:

Fundamental 1. Get the key moments right

Fundamental 2. Align the key moments

Fundamental 3. Identify the critical event

Fundamental 4. Assist the customer

FUNDAMENTAL 1. GET THE KEY MOMENTS RIGHT

In an effort for you to instinctively recognize these moments, we first present them from the seller's perspective.

Table 5.1 Key moments that matter from a seller's perspective

Key Moments	Seller's Perspective
#1 Outreach	The first time a customer hears from you, initiated by you, designed to help the customer realize they have a problem. It can take the form of an ad, an outbound email, a thought provoking blog post, a cold call, and so on.
#2 First contact	This is usually the first person-to-person communication, often in the form of an email exchange followed up with a call. Its goal is to find out more information about the customer and their problem and qualify them.
#3 Discovery	The discovery meeting is designed to diagnose the customer's problem and share how your product or service can be used as a solution. Sometimes the discovery is combined with a product demonstration.
#4 Close	The discussions that happen as the customer prepares to commit to your product or service.
#5 Kick-off	Also called onboarding, the meeting in which the customer is set up with your product or service and you both agree to a plan for how to achieve the desired impact.
#6 Review	Sometimes called the Executive Business Review, this meeting is a check-in to ensure usage of the product and that the problem is being solved and the customer is getting the intended results from your product or service.
#7 Renew	This is closely associated with the Upsell or Cross-sell meeting if the customer is getting results from the relationship, if they are likely to renew and with it increase the lifetime value of the customer. Another way of increasing lifetime value is to use more of your product and/or use it across a broader part of a customer's organization.

Remember that we specified that the moments that matter above are from the seller's perspective? That's important because getting the moments that matter right are all about looking at it from the buyer's perspective. We have found that much of what traditional sales teaches us to do in the moments that matter is counterproductive because it is from a seller's point of view. Let's review the moments that matter from a buyer's perspective.

Table 5.2 Key moments that matter from a buyer's perspective

Key Moments	Buyer's Perspective
#1 Outreach	Reach out to me because you noticed I (am going to) have a pain.
#2 First contact	Have a conversation with me to gain a better understanding of my situation.
#3 Discovery	Diagnose and demo the impact of your product based on my situation.
#4 Close	Help me sell this internally and make a trade-off to match my budget.
#5 Kick-off	Orchestrate the next 90/180 days to ensure it works as advertised.
#6 Review	Measure and ensure that the promised impact is achieved.
#7 Renew	Grow by helping identify other areas where similar impact can be created.

FUNDAMENTAL 2. ALIGN THE KEY MOMENTS

If you look at the aforementioned moments, they are all centered around the same concept: Creating a positive impact on the customer's business. To be successful, you have to orient your organization around the moments that matter, and have those moments be aligned around the impact your solution offers a customer. However, a customer does not experience a lack of impact; instead, they experience a problem or a pain as a symptom.

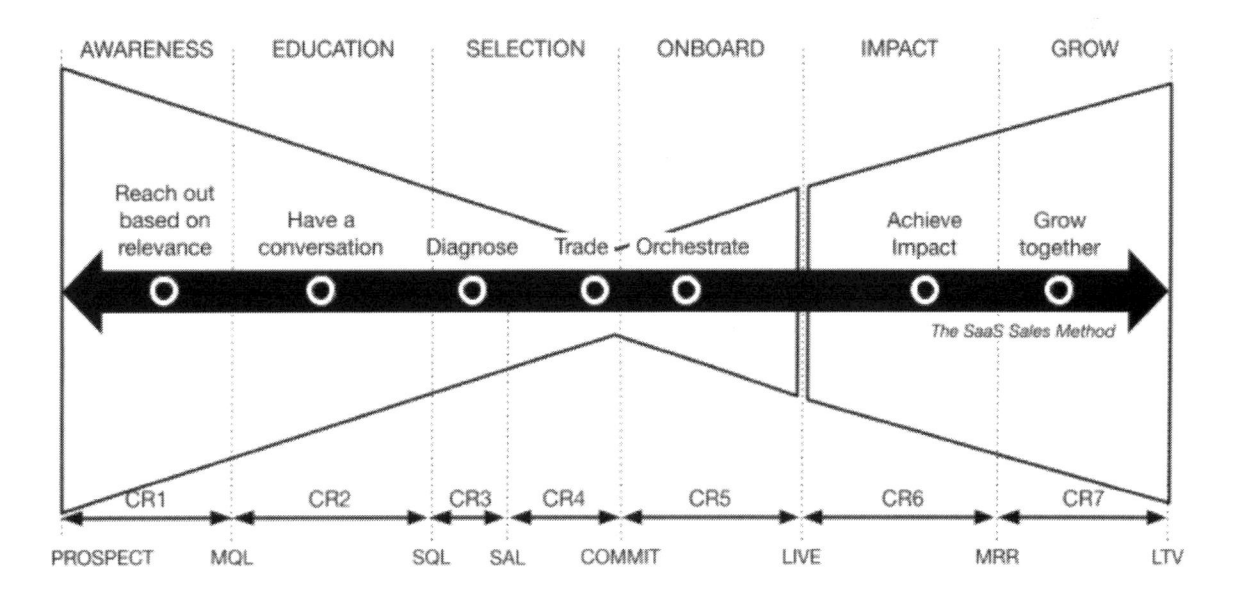

Figure 5.1 Moments that matter from a customer perspective, align using the impact journey

Emotional versus Rational Impact

There are two ways that impact is perceived: rational, which is measurable using facts and figures; and emotional, which is about feelings and experiences. For example, when a customer says, *"The reports are giving me a headache."*

Research shows that people tend to make an emotional decision then validate that decision with facts and figures. In Figure 5.2, you will notice that to understand the impact; you will have to go through layers, like an onion. To peel away each of these layers, you need to master the art of asking questions. The true rational and emotional impact often lies several layers deep and will require a series of questions to uncover.

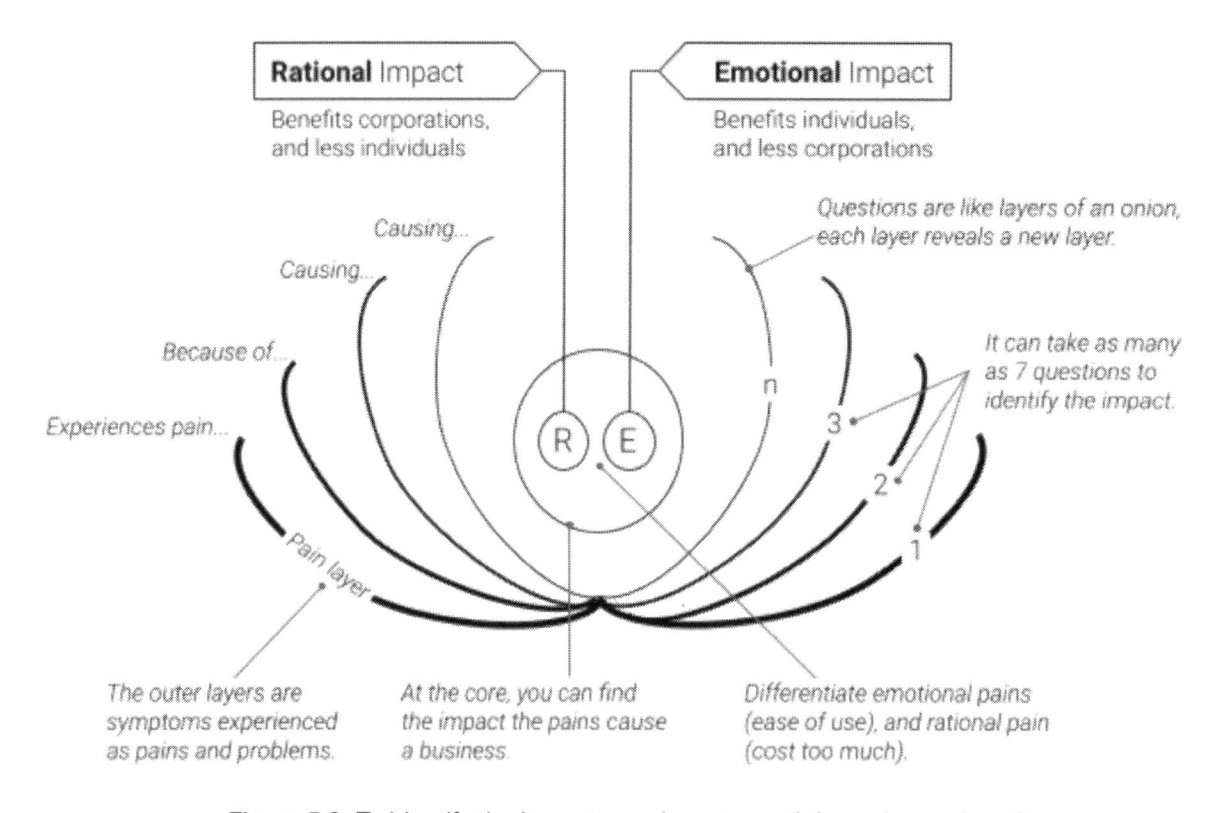

Figure 5.2 To identify the impact, you have to peel through a series of layers

Although emotional impact helps the end customer have a better experience, it often looks and feels like a cost reduction solution. Examples include easier-to-understand dashboards, fewer clicks, finding better candidates quicker, and so on.

There are two key differentiators between emotional and rational impact:
- Emotional impact first benefits a person; rational impact first benefits a corporation

- Emotional impact such as ease-of-use follows the laws of habit formation which means it is harder to change the longer a customer uses it

Thus, don't just rely on improving ROI; also try to find other types of impact your customer cares about. There are different ways your value proposition has an impact on your client's business. You need to know which type of impact is most important to your customer.

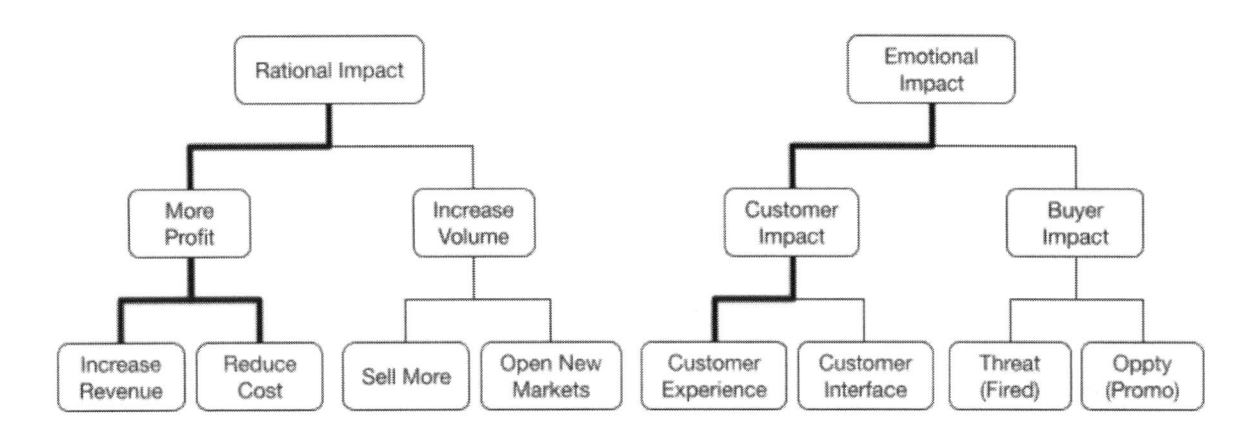

Figure 5.3 The most common types of impact

The most common impacts are:

Increase Revenue The need to grow often outshines cost reduction because most companies are so heavily focused on growth and increasing the value of the business. It is no surprise that products that increase revenue enjoy shorter sales cycles and can be sold at a higher price.

Reduce Cost A solution that increases revenue hinges on an effectiveness driven model. Compare this to a solution that reduces cost, which hinges on an efficiency-driven value proposition. Buying a solution that reduces cost is the easier choice to make for a decision maker; however, these solutions are often price-competitive, and this makes the business dependent on deal volume.

Improve Customer Experience Improving the customer experience and/or interaction results in productivity improvement, and it often looks and feels like a cost reduction solution. Examples include easier to understand dashboards, easier to operate tools, improved collaboration, reduced risk, and so on. Collaboration products, productivity tools, business intelligence software, human resources information systems, security products...all of these fit into this category.

Each of these approaches can lead to a healthy business, but it is important to be upfront with your client on what impact you can and will be delivering, and at what time. Let's discuss that next.

FUNDAMENTAL 3. IDENTIFY THE CRITICAL EVENT

Just providing impact is not good enough. Impact is a function of time. In the figure below, you will notice that over time, a priority increases from nice-to-have to want-to-have, and at one point, even reaches need-to-have. Sales organizations must excel at determining where clients and customers are on this horizon. As the priority drops, a customer may go dark leading you to believe that the "budget is spent," not realizing that the conditions may soon change in your favor.

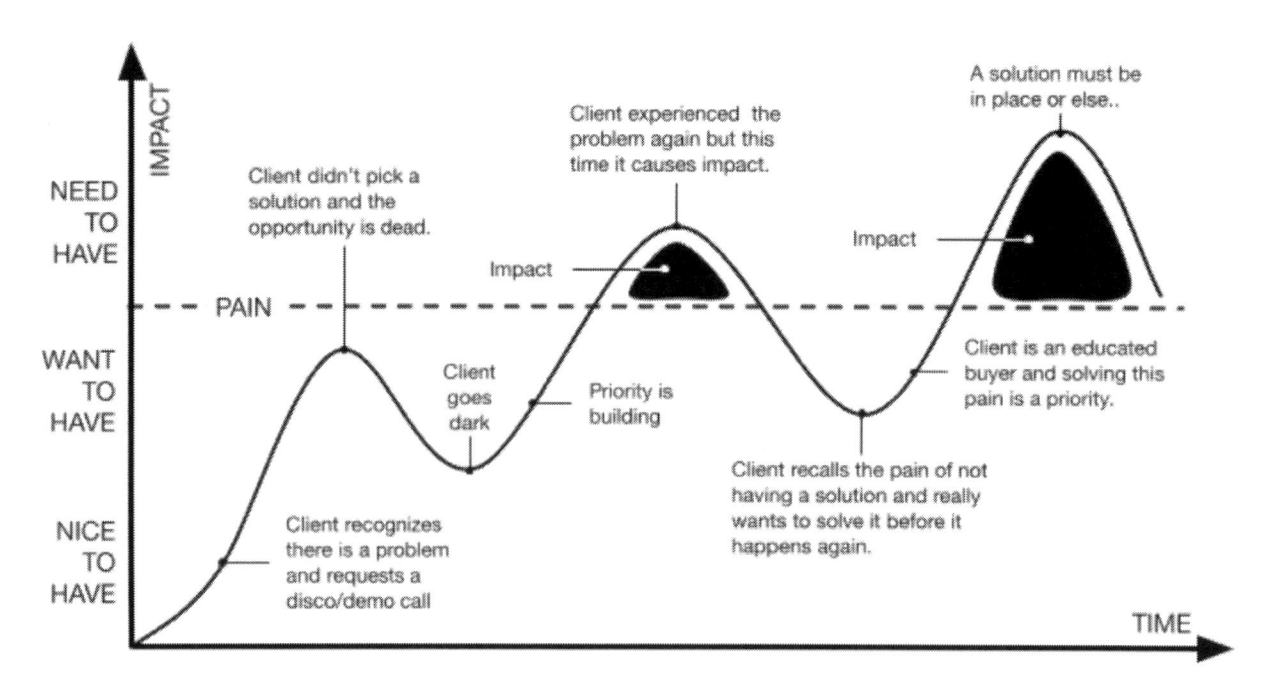

Figure 5.4 Priority is a function of impact over time

To uncover a critical event, you need to train your team that whenever a client mentions a date, they should ask the question, *"May I ask what happens if you miss that date?"* This question will point back to the impact, and implies that impact and critical event go together.

A common misconception in SaaS relates to when a customer says, *"We have no budget."* A SaaS prospect hardly ever has a budget issue, but rather a time issue. Your service simply is not a priority at this time.

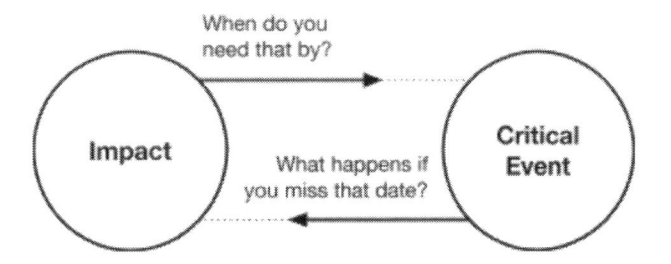

Figure 5.5 The direct relationship between impact and critical event

Solving a priority issue is very different from solving a non-priority issue as the impact of your service fluctuates over time. If your solution does not provide a meaningful impact, it will never become a priority.

Case in point: Take for example selling an Applicant Tracking System. If your customer hires three to four people a year, it may not provide enough impact to be a priority. However, when the recruiting corporation receives funding and suddenly needs to hire 20 people in 30 days, with 10 every month thereafter, there is a need for the applicant tracking system. The opening of the job requisitions is then what we refer to as a **critical event date**. It is a date so important it literally drives the timeline of the decision. You cannot create a customer's critical event, you can only discover it.

FUNDAMENTAL 4. ASSIST THE CLIENT TO BUY

Most clients have an arbitrary decision process in which they go through the following steps:

- **Step 1. Inquire** with a variety of stakeholders in their company about the decision criteria;

- **Step 2. Identify** options to address these decision criteria such as competitors and substitutes;

- **Step 3. Establish** the rank of each option against the decision criteria based on research. This could include gauging the ability to execute based on analyst reports or on obtaining customer feedback via a public review site;

Despite this process, clients invariably identify price as a top criterion.

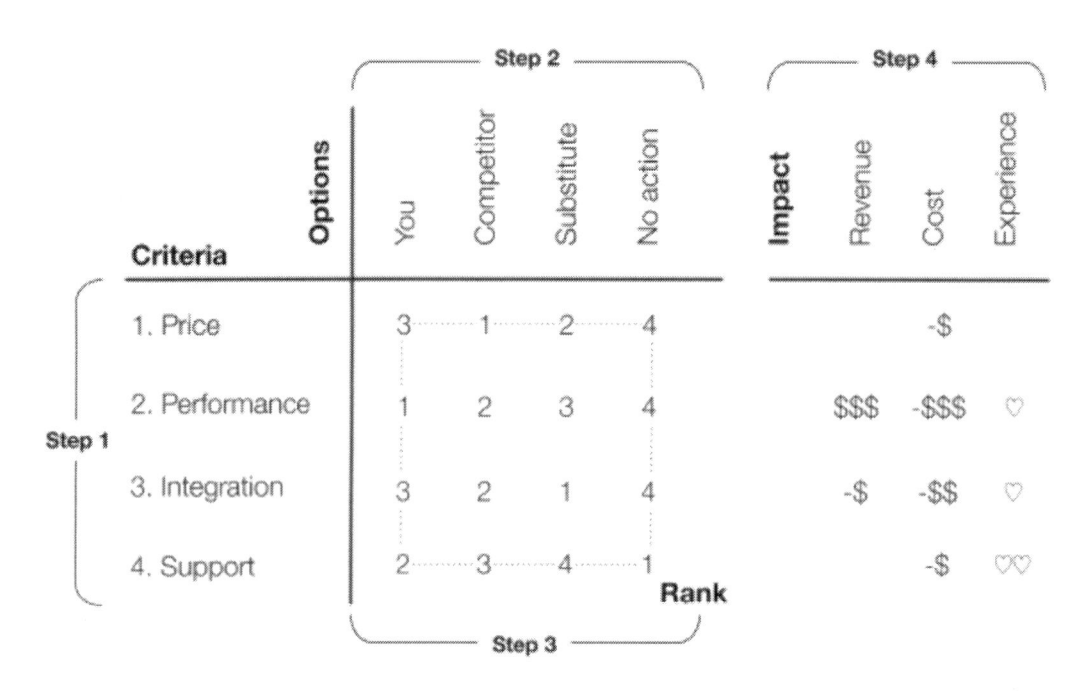

Figure 5.6 Trade-off metrics and the steps used to make an educated decision

Educated buyers, however, are able to gauge the impact of each criterion and decide on the right solution based on the impact it provides to their business - not just price. As a sales professional, you may have to guide the customer on the decision criteria that they should use. The challenge is to help the customer uncover the impact of each decision criterion.

Step 4. Determine the impact of each criterion.

In Figure 5.7 example, the impact is measured by determining the increase in revenue, reduction in cost, or improvement in customer experience. For example, your service may "cost" $500/month more. However, your product may offer an increased performance that provides $2,000/month or $24,000 per year of additional revenue.

This should prioritize the impact of the revenue increase from the product's *performance* over the impact of the reduction in *price*. The salesperson doing this dozens of times a week or month is the expert and should, on merit, convince the customer of the impact.

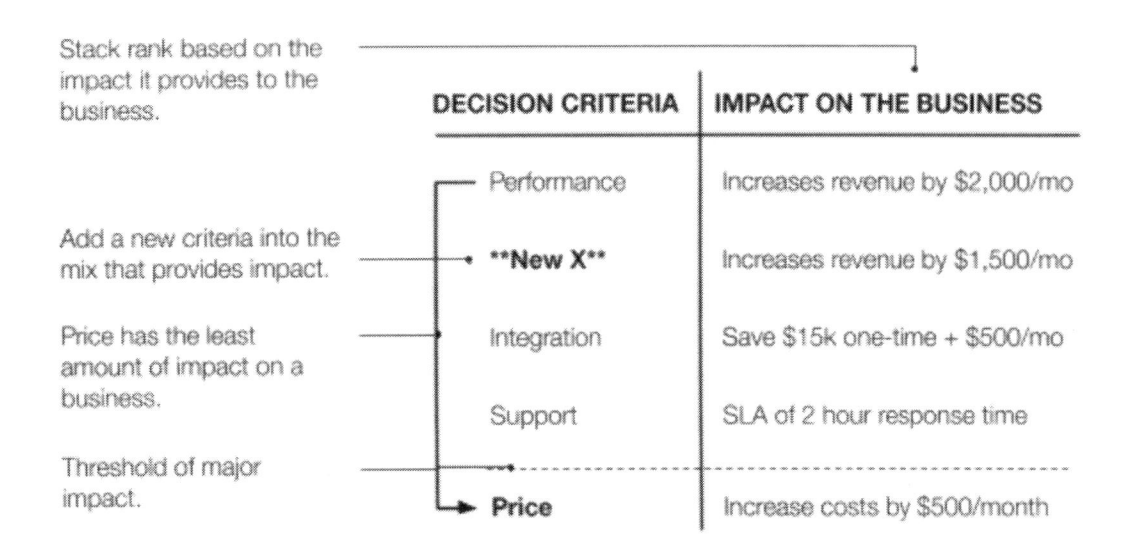

	DECISION CRITERIA	IMPACT ON THE BUSINESS
Stack rank based on the impact it provides to the business.	Performance	Increases revenue by $2,000/mo
Add a new criteria into the mix that provides impact.	**New X**	Increases revenue by $1,500/mo
Price has the least amount of impact on a business.	Integration	Save $15k one-time + $500/mo
	Support	SLA of 2 hour response time
Threshold of major impact.	Price	Increase costs by $500/month

Figure 5.7 Demonstrating the impact of each criterion

Through proper discovery, you can educate the customer on what is important for them, then trust that a well-educated customer will make the right decision for their business.

RECAP CHAPTER 5 | **MOMENTS THAT MATTER**

There are a few special moments that you need to pay attention to because they are important to the customer. These are called the Moments That Matter.

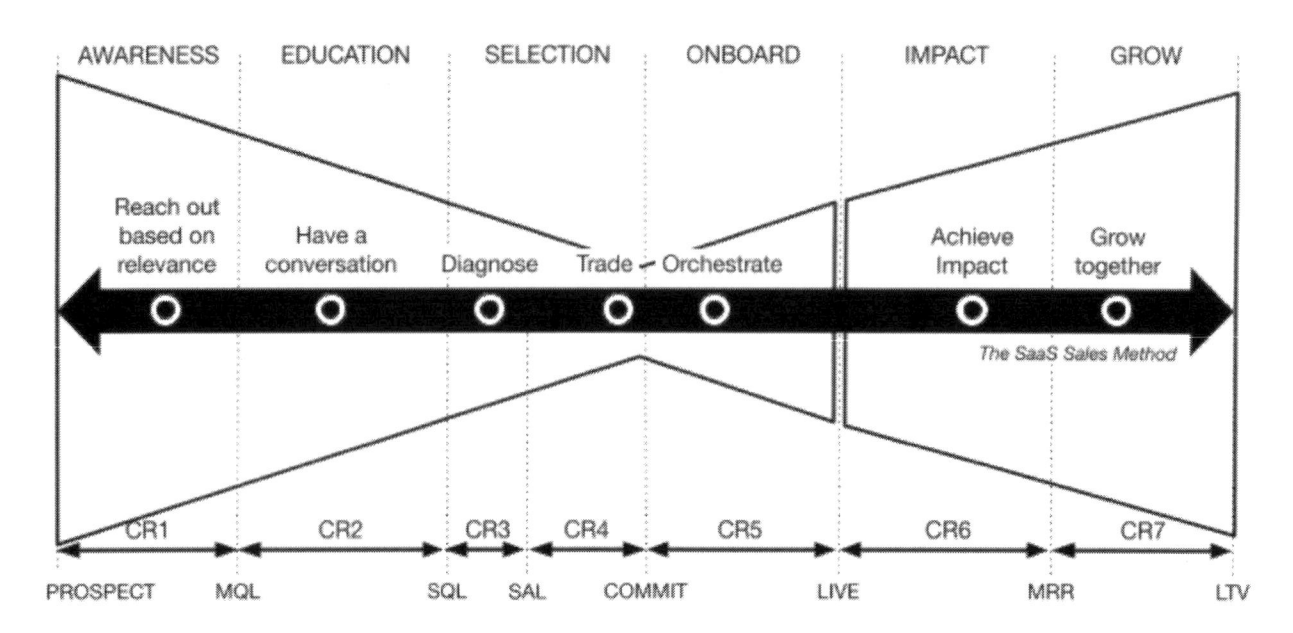

To get these moments to work in concert, you have to get the fundamentals right:

Fundamental 1. Get the right key moments from the customer's perspective

Fundamental 2. Align the key moments around impact on the customer's business

Fundamental 3. Identify a critical event to achieve the impact

Fundamental 4. Assist the customer with decision criteria based on impact

Now that we have identified the moments that matter and how to make them work in concert, we are going to share examples of how to improve each. As we know from the previous chapter, a 10% improvement across seven key moments results in twice the revenue.

CHAPTER 6
BLUEPRINTS

The goals of the blueprints we provide are simple: create a framework (not a script) of how to perform a set of actions during a moment that matters. Then over time, improve each of these frameworks until they work at their absolute best. However, before we share some of these blueprints, we want to provide a guideline that we have found to be critical in today's communication.

Your interest in helping a customer resolve their problem has to be authentic.

It cannot be manufactured, and you should not use authenticity as a trick to close a deal. More and more, marketing organizations are making authenticity a concept, they recommend the use of certain words, record videos on your LinkedIn, etc. We do not believe this is sustainable. We have found that if you follow the next five principles, you are genuinely authentic and not fabricating it.

Principle 1. **Understand their pain** Do your research and only reach out to those who have a pain or to whom you think you can help avoid it. Do not reach out to people who are "just a fit"

Principle 2. **First emotional, *then* rational** Understand that generally, emotional impact benefits people first, and rational impact benefits companies first. Focus first on the emotional impact.

Principle 3. **Educate, do not pitch** Trust that if you educate the customer, they will make the best decision. Therefore, help your customer think through the problem they are experiencing, and share best practices of others who experienced the same.

Principle 4. **Assist the buying process** People hate being sold to, but they love to buy. So why don't we stop the selling and, instead, focus on helping them to buy.

Principle 5. **Provide value in every interaction** Don't just do check-ins; provide value in every interaction with every client, every time. Offer market information, insights, use-cases and whatever else you can to add value.

If you master the above principles, you will be genuinely authentic, not because it helps you close a deal, but because during the process of executing the above principles, you have become someone who cares.

We have identified the Moments that Matter, and aligned them along impact as discussed in Chapter 5. Next, we are connecting each Moment to a corresponding conversion metric we discussed in Chapter 4. We can now provide a series of examples of specific actions your customer-facing teams can take during these moments to improve the respective conversion rate by 10%. And as we now know, a 10% improvement across seven key Moments results in twice the revenue.

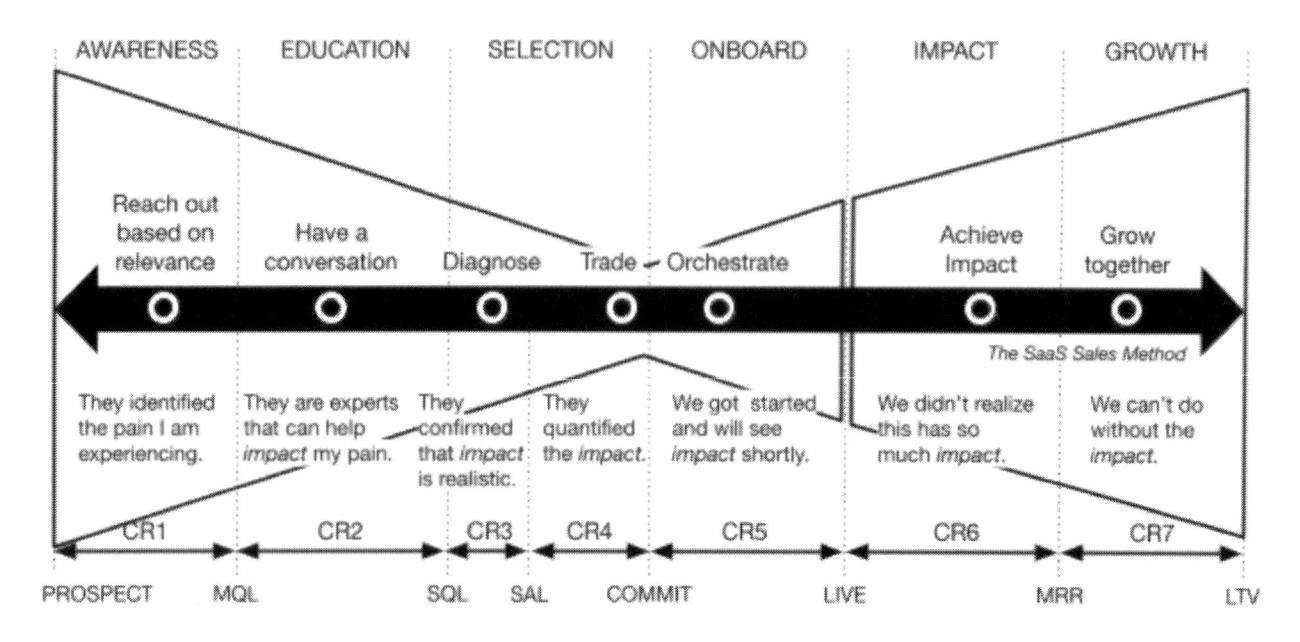

Figure 6.1 Key Moments that Matter, the impact journey, and the corresponding conversion metrics

The seven key Moments we are going to focus on:

1. Reach out based on a pain they may have, and be relevant to them from the first interaction
2. Have a conversation as a human being, not as a sales qualifier
3. Perform a diagnosis on the client's situation before you prescribe a solution
4. Trade, don't negotiate: maintain value for your product by trading items of equal value
5. Orchestrate, don't onboard: redo the deal until the client is signed
6. Achieve impact, don't pursue usage: look for both the emotional and rational impact
7. Grow in different areas: renew, upsell, resell, and cross-sell

MOMENT #1: REACH OUT TO CLIENTS WHO HAVE A PAIN

When we ask our clients who their prospects are, they often mention a job title in a vertical market, such as the CTO at a financial institution. Many companies buy and/or create a list of prospects that hold a title, in a vertical market, in a region, of a certain size. They then enrich that contact data with email addresses, telephone numbers, and social handles. This allows them to create a personalized outreach email, at scale, like the one in the next example. The thing about this email, which is quite representative of today's sales organizations, is that it is the result of correlation, not causation.

> Sample 6.1 Correlation-based outreach with the aim of setting a meeting
>
> *Dear {{ first name }},*
>
> *I noticed on LinkedIn that you are the {{ job title }} at {{ company name }}. The reason I am reaching out to you is that others in your industry such as {{ client first name }} at {{ company name }} ran into {{ problem }}.*
>
> *Attached is a {{ use-case }} that describes how {{ our company name }} helped him/her solve this by {{ doing this }} and how it {{ caused xx% increase }}.*
>
> *Can we meet for 15 minutes to discuss how we can help you?*
>
> *<Close>*

However, when we ask the CTO why they signed up for our service, we learn that it was because earlier in the year they suffered a security breach. The fact that they were a bank was pure coincidence, and thus correlated with their profile, but not caused by it. What that means is that for this seller, any other institution that had a breach should be a prospect – they should not target only banks!

This allows us to rewrite the outbound email based on causation instead of correlation:

> Sample 6.2 Causation-based outreach with the aim of providing impact
>
> *Dear {{ first name }},*
>
> *In your recent article, you mentioned that your infrastructure was breached.*
>
> *Please find attached a use-case from two weeks ago. On page two, I highlighted how the headaches of a similar breach can be avoided based on a best practice discovered by {{ first name }} at {{ company }}.*
>
> *{{ first name }}, let me know if you would like to talk to one of our experts on this?*
>
> *<Close>*

Reaching out to a client using a provocative statement takes a lot of preparation - but like a song, a book, or a movie, there is a blueprint for success.

We can use this to develop turn-by-turn directions for how to create a provocative statement:

Blueprint 6.1 How to reach out using a provocative statement, rich in relevance and genuinely authentic

Step 1. Pick one of your own accounts and perform research

Step 2. Pick a value prop and use-case that applies to the client (the person, not the company)

Step 3. Research the current situation through online search

Step 4. Outline specifics of the new situation without overtly mentioning your products or terms unique to you

Step 5. Identify a critical date such as a product launch, or an event (such as, to reach one million users)

Step 6. Establish rational and emotional impact based on the selected value prop; ensure you have a use-case (proof) of a relevant client (size, location, market, etc.)

Current situation: Demonstrate you have done research
" In your recent 10Q statement, I noticed you are spending $10M/year on IT. Talking to Peter on your IT team, I learned you are using an on-premise solution changing to a cloud solution.

Relevance: Indicate this to be relevant.

New situation: Don't mention a product name.

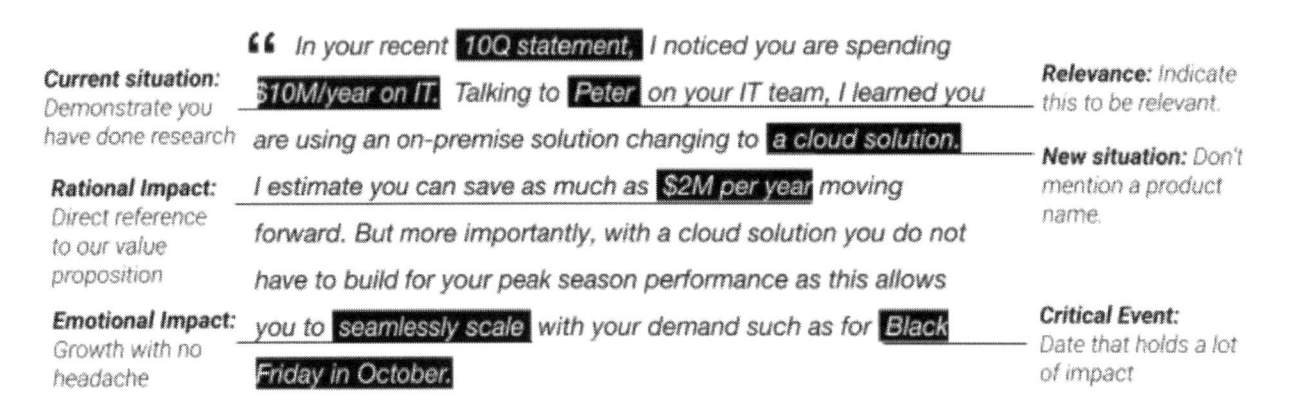

Rational Impact: Direct reference to our value proposition
I estimate you can save as much as $2M per year moving forward. But more importantly, with a cloud solution you do not have to build for your peak season performance as this allows

Emotional Impact: Growth with no headache
you to seamlessly scale with your demand such as for Black Friday in October.

Critical Event: Date that holds a lot of impact

Figure 6.2 Blueprint of a provocative statement

The caveat here is that, as professionals, we all receive dozens of emails every day that provide no value. Therefore, even the cold outbound email we described in the example above may soon be a thing of the past. In fact, as we write, the EU's GDPR is being put in place, which may legally limit what can be done with outbound email. Regardless of GDPR rules though, in practice, low email open rates are taking their toll on outbound campaigns worldwide, and that is even *if* those campaigns are well-written and based on causation, as we recommend.

MOMENT #2: CONVERSATION, NOT QUALIFICATION

One of the first things all salespeople are taught is qualification. This is the task of determining if a person representing a company with characteristics (such as size, market, and intent to purchase) qualifies them to continue in the sales process.

When we were selling IBM mainframe computers, this made a lot of sense. There were only a few mainframes to go around, and everyone wanted them. However, the cost of selling those computers added up to tens of thousands of dollars per sale, with access to specialized resources such as engineers and architects that provided their expertise on integration into the customer's infrastructure. Sales reps had to use a defined set of questions to extract concessions from a customer and, based on the answers, determine if this was a *priority for the seller.* In today's world, a SaaS solution can be integrated into a cloud platform sometimes with a single click, or the provision of a login via a simple email. Outdated qualification methods designed around multimillion dollar products do not apply to high velocity sales. The client today has lots of options, and securing budget is often no longer an issue for them.

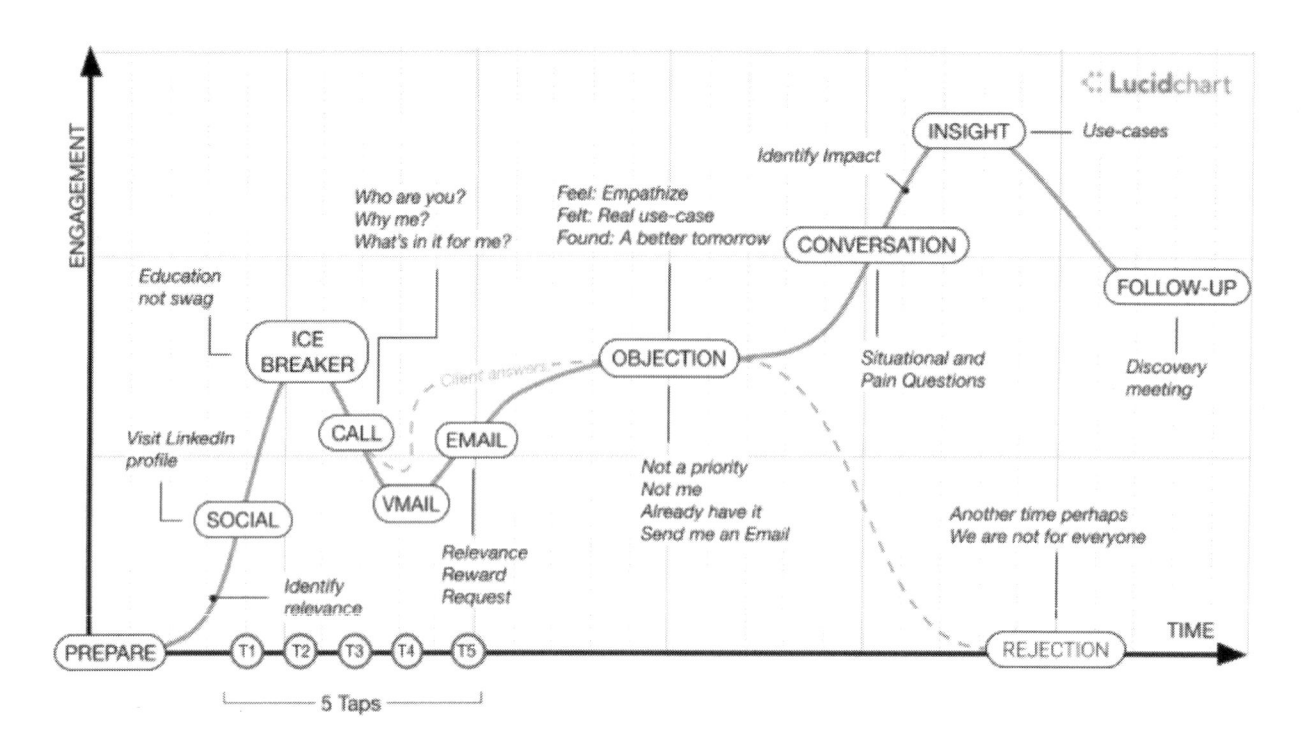

Figure 6.2a How to apply TALKER conversation techniques to initial customer calls

So instead of qualification, we recommend the fundamental skill of conversation to establish the priority and the impact the client is looking to achieve. The framework for teaching conversation skills is built on an easy to remember acronym, TALKER.

Blueprint 6.2 How to have a sincere conversation

Step 1. Tone of voice, not just how we use our actual voice, but the use of written tone and emojis in chat and email. One of the key elements of tone is speed - for example, not talking too fast in person, but responding very fast in chat.

Step 2. Ask questions. Master not only closed- and open-ended questions, but also learn to ask diagnostic questions like a doctor would.

Step 3. Listen actively to patterns in the customer's words, their tone, and even their emotional state. Learn how to recognize emotional words.

Step 4. Keep accurate but brief notes, differentiating situation, pain, and impact while identifying causality.

Step 5. Elaborate and follow the thread of a conversation while teasing out pain and impact.

Step 6. Repeat what you've heard to ensure you understand what is being said.

A conversation is a more natural, more human thing. It connects with the prospect on an emotional level and tries to further uncover their real, pressing problem. It is the moment in which a hypothesis about customer impact can be fleshed out by a trained professional. As you can see in the next blueprint, we can apply TALKER in all kinds of Moments to start a conversation by email, phone, and social interactions.

Coming out of this Moment, you should have a very clear idea of whether and how your product can impact the customer's business. More importantly, you should have managed the conversation in a way the customer themselves have verbalized the problem and envisioned a potential solution for themselves.

Take [Get a Meeting]

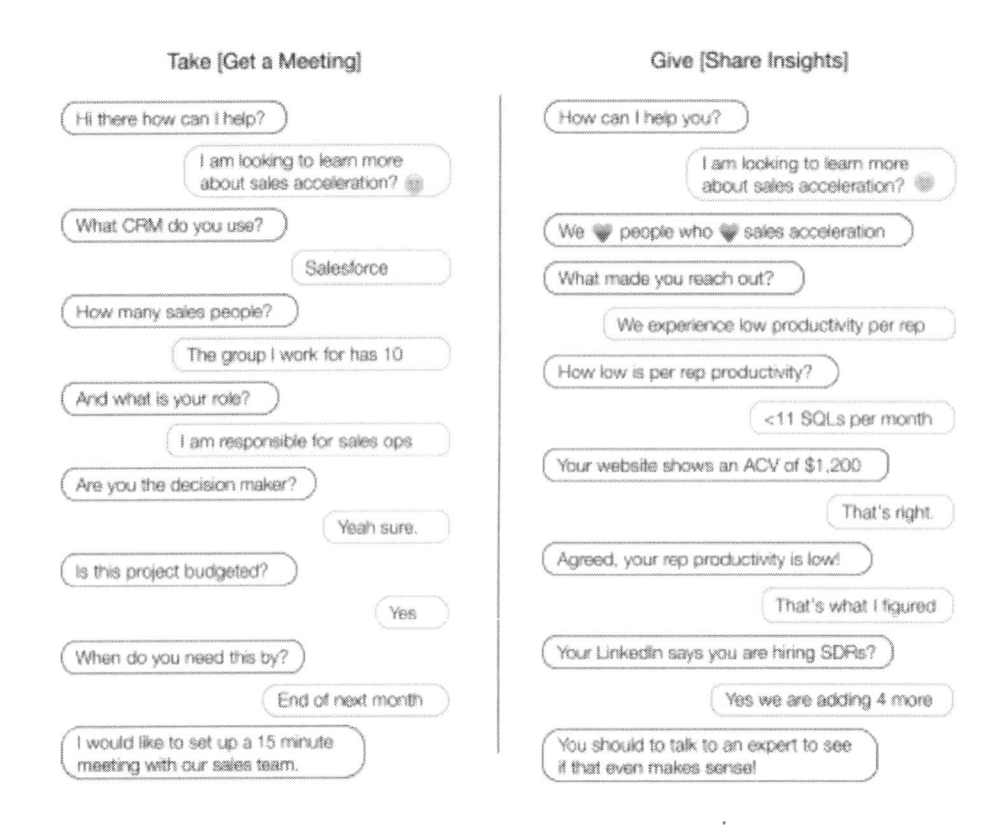

- Hi there how can I help?
- I am looking to learn more about sales acceleration?
- What CRM do you use?
- Salesforce
- How many sales people?
- The group I work for has 10
- And what is your role?
- I am responsible for sales ops
- Are you the decision maker?
- Yeah sure.
- Is this project budgeted?
- Yes
- When do you need this by?
- End of next month
- I would like to set up a 15 minute meeting with our sales team.

Give [Share Insights]

- How can I help you?
- I am looking to learn more about sales acceleration?
- We ♥ people who ♥ sales acceleration
- What made you reach out?
- We experience low productivity per rep
- How low is per rep productivity?
- <11 SQLs per month
- Your website shows an ACV of $1,200
- That's right.
- Agreed, your rep productivity is low!
- That's what I figured
- Your LinkedIn says you are hiring SDRs?
- Yes we are adding 4 more
- You should to talk to an expert to see if that even makes sense!

Figure 6.2b Example of a live chat with a client who came to your website to learn more

MOMENT #3: DIAGNOSIS BEFORE PRESCRIPTION

We often tell our own clients that *prescription before diagnosis is malpractice*. We're not the first to say it, and that is because it is very, very true. In the moment of education, the customer already realizes they have a problem. Using a medical analogy, the customer is like a patient who is complaining of symptoms. At this point, it is the job of the salesperson to further dial in on the root cause of those symptoms by performing a diagnosis. A diagnosis can be performed during a discovery call or a demo (or both). It can be done in one meeting, or across multiple meetings.

DIAGNOSIS THROUGH DISCOVERY

The more a salesperson can do to understand the customer's pain and the potential business impact, the better they will be able to actually recommend a solution based on the company's products, which can have an impact on the customer's problem.

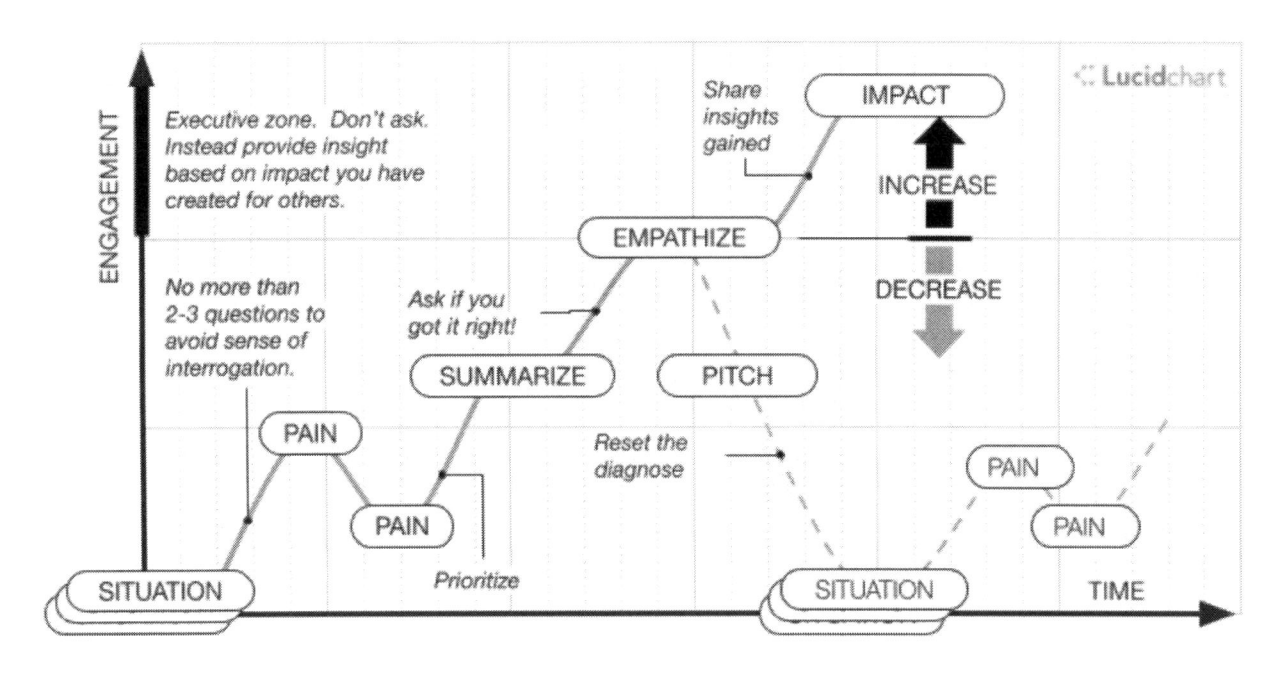

Figure 6.3a How to have a conversation

For diagnosing, we use a question-based framework used by all kinds of professionals to understand their clients quickly, from emergency responders to your favorite car mechanic.

Blueprint 6.3a How to perform a diagnosis

Step 1. First ask two or three questions to learn the context of the situation

Step 2. Then ask a few questions to understand the pain[1]

Step 3. Summarize: "So you have [this situation] and [that situation] causing you [this pain], did I get that right?"

Step 4. Empathize with "I hear this a lot," or "You are not alone in this."

Step 5. Identify both the emotional and rational impact

Step 6. Establish the critical event

DIAGNOSE THROUGH DEMONSTRATION

In a high velocity sale, you might find a client who really wants a quick demo. This does not mean you can make it a pitch-fest. It does mean that you need to integrate your diagnosis

---

[1] Two books that capture question based sales techniques are "The Secrets of Question Based Selling" by Thomas Freese and the wildly popular "SPIN Selling" by Neil Rackham from the Huthwaite Institute. We encourage all your customer facing teams to master questions based techniques.

into the demo and ensure your demo is relevant for the client. Give yourself an opportunity to obtain valuable information, such as the impact your product can have on the client's business.

It is not uncommon for a demo to turn into a monologue that lasts anywhere from 10 to 40 minutes. And it cannot be a surprise that customers lose interest when there is too much information to which they cannot relate. At the same time, the sales rep is missing a golden opportunity to learn about their challenges and the impact their service could have on their business.

The next figure visualizes the engagement during the demo.

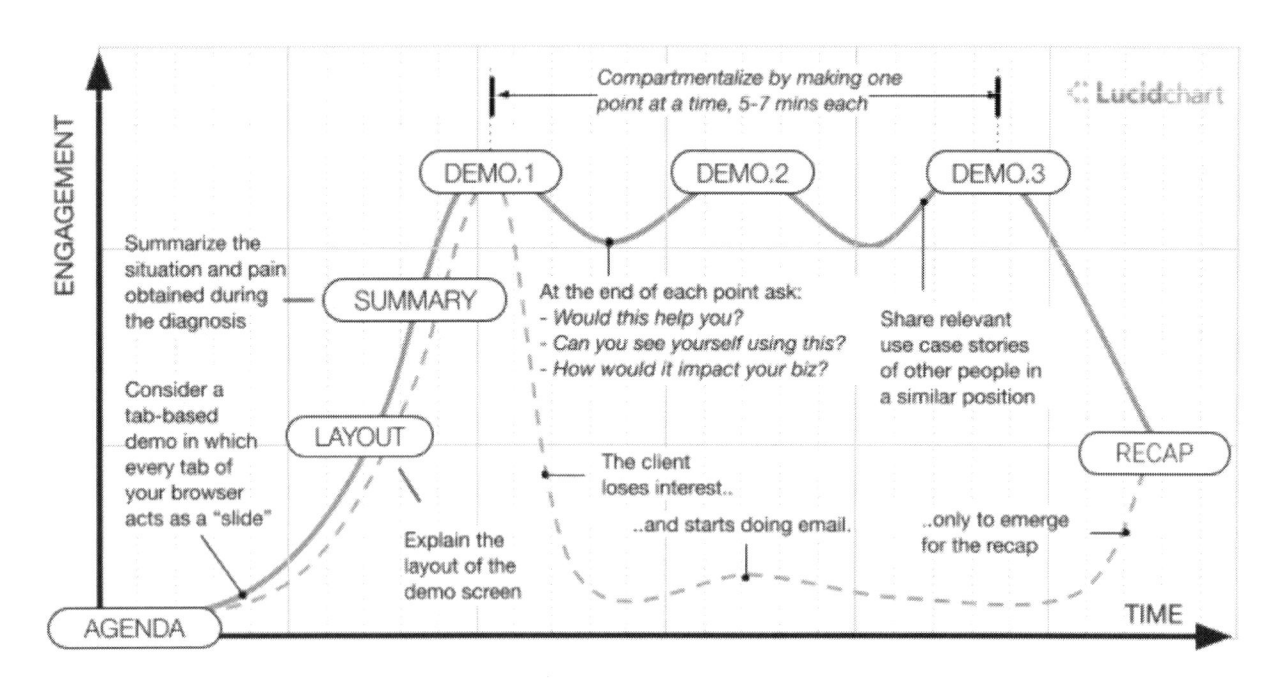

Figure 6.3b How to diagnose while performing a demonstration

Blueprint 6.3b How to perform a demonstration

Step 1. Write an agenda of the points you are going to demo; keep it to three points on a 30 minute call, and five points on a 60 minute call

Step 2. For each demo point, summarize your previous diagnosis and point out why you are showing this particular page, dashboard, or feature of your product

Step 3. Orient the client with the layout of your product on the screen

Step 4. Then demonstrate:
- In the customer's context, how your product solves their problem

- "Hand over" controls by asking if there is anything they would like to see
- Identify impact for each point by asking the following three questions:

  "Would this address the issue you described earlier?"
  "Can you see yourself using this product?"
  "How would this impact your business?"

Step 5. At the end of each, summarize the key findings, and move to the next point

Step 6. Following the demonstration, recap the findings across all three points using the customer vernacular

MOMENT #4: TRADE, NOT NEGOTIATE

This single change in wording and emphasis has one of the greatest effects on cumulative sales in all of our work. Here's how it goes:

When salespeople negotiate, they tend to think in terms of numbers and percentages moving up and down. In a high velocity sale, we notice that they often discount quickly and in large increments. As a result, they often give away discounts far more than they should, and for little in return.

A company with an innovative SaaS product with an annual contract value (ACV) of $12,000 should increase its price annually by at least 8% given its rapid product development. By giving a 20% discount during negotiation, an inexperienced negotiator may view this as "only $2,400", however this adds up over three years to be $10,920, or nearly one year of revenue. And for what? Most deals that reach the negotiation stage seldom turn on price. Instead, we encourage organizations to think of negotiation as trading, of discounts as price adjustments, and to make these price adjustments small.

In trading, both parties give up something of value in order to be better off. By definition, trading is win-win. What do they trade for? There are any number of things a customer can do or say that will significantly help a business. References, case studies, social media mentions, PR quotes, and all kinds of other items can form a menu of trading options at different levels of price adjustment.

What this also does is put a price on discounts, and everyone knows what happens when we pay attention to the price of something: its value becomes clear. So, when a customer isn't willing to do a PR mention and turns down the discount, the average discount rate for the team goes down. This single change has caused the average discount rate offered by the teams we train from above 20% to below 10%. That is revenue that goes straight to the bottom line.

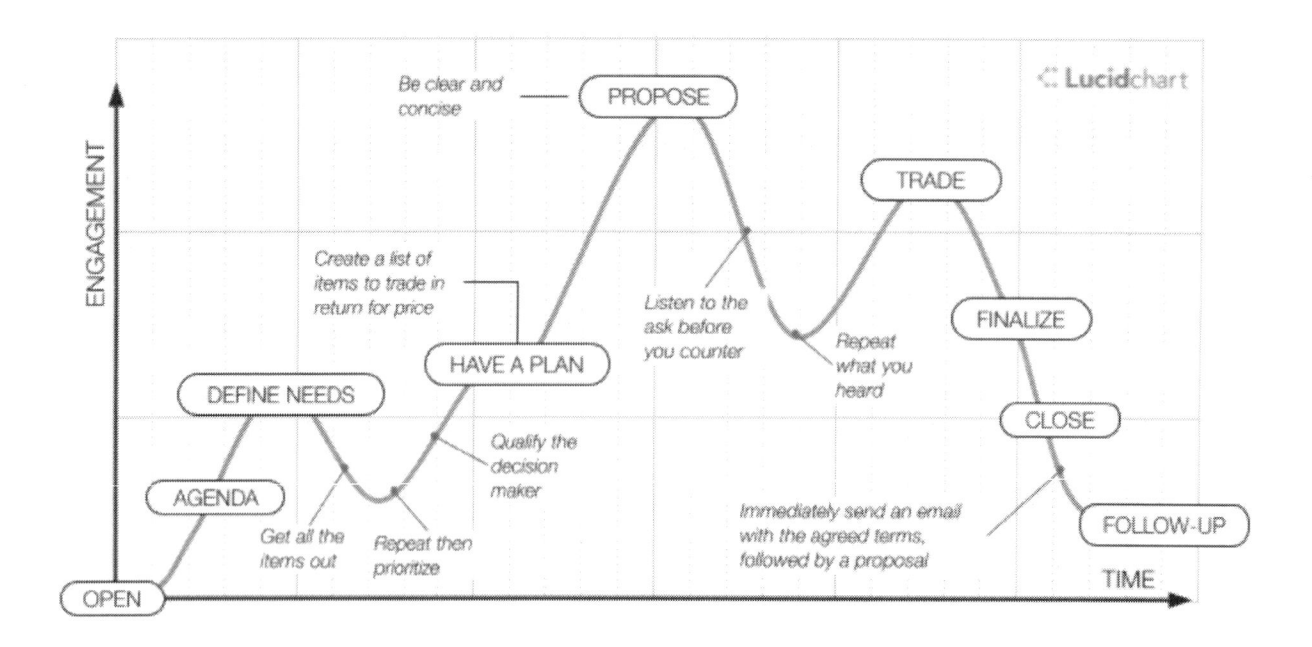

Figure 6.4 How to have a conversation

Blueprint 6.4 The Trade Framework

Step 1. Know the person on the other side of the table, their way of responding, etc.

Step 2. Understand the situation: what is the desired impact, and the critical event?

Step 3. Prepare a list of trade items and understand the value of each one.

Step 4. Ensure that you understand all the elements of the offer.

Step 5. Get all negotiation items on the table, i.e., price, terms, setup fee, etc.

Step 6. Repeat/Ask what you heard, "So if I'm getting this right, you want ___ . Is there anything else?"

Step 7. Prioritize the issues: "Let me ask, what is most important to you: Price or...?"

Step 8. Before you make the offer, be sure you are talking to the decision maker. *"If we come to an agreement, can you make the decision by {today}?"*

Step 9. Make the offer, do not hesitate. Be clear and be concise.

Step 10. Listen and repeat the counter-offer.

MOMENT #5: ORCHESTRATE, NOT ONBOARD

Onboarding is a term that has lost its meaning through overuse.

Everyone thinks they know what it means, which usually comes down to something like "getting the customer set up with the product." While the technical setup may be the immediate concern in the minds of both the seller and the buyer, it does not cover the larger missed opportunity that this first customer interaction after selection represents. The relationship before and after the commitment has undergone a fundamental change. Before a commitment was struck, the buyer did not want to provide too much insight because they feared losing leverage. Similarly, the seller may not have been completely transparent on how things really work.

However, after the contract is signed, the buyer is often willing to provide a lot more insights to ensure success. This may even involve an adjusted timeline, additional budget, and access to previously inaccessible executives. This window of mutual openness is only available for a short while, and missing it will often limit the opportunity even before it has started.

So instead of just onboarding the customer into the product, this Moment should be treated as an opportunity to orchestrate the entire business relationship from that point forward. It is during onboarding, while the customer is vested in a successful outcome, that the opportunity exists to set expectations about how the product will impact the customer, how it is measured, and to define what it *means* so it can be easily communicated later on. When a revenue organization re-frames onboarding into orchestration, it becomes a business and a strategic discussion rather than just a technical one. Keep in mind that this may require you to treat this as two different discussions: the more strategic one, which is business-focused, and the technical one, which is more tactical in nature.

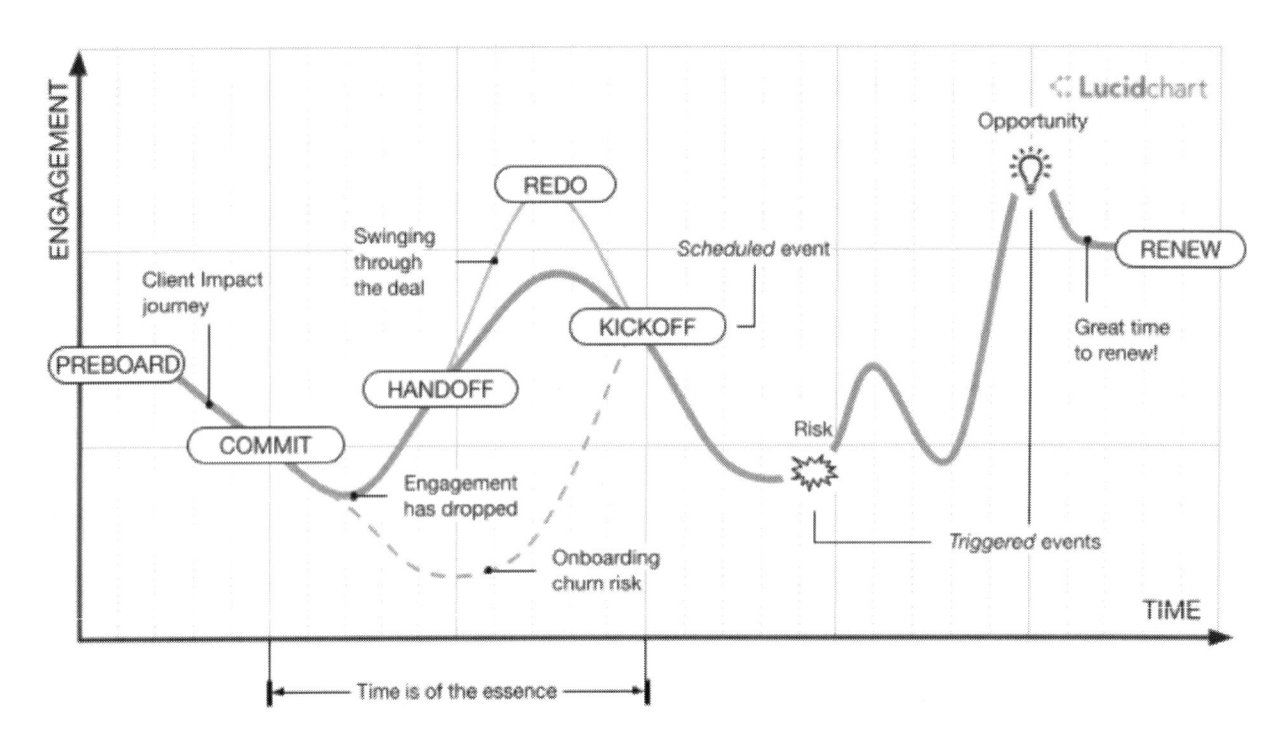

Figure 6.6 How to orchestrate the impact journey using handoff, redo and kickoff

What the business conversation allows is for the seller to guide how the relationship will develop over the months to come, to set the milestones by which the customer judges success, and ultimately to set up the relationship so that it has a real impact on the customer's business.

Blueprint 6.5 The orchestration consisting of the handoff, the redo and the kick-off

Step 1. Hand off the deal to the CSM/Onboarder using impact and critical event details

- Sales stays involved after the deal is closed, ensuring smooth hand-off
- Time is of the essence; provide short, frequent communication with updates

Step 2. Redo the deal. Since the relationship has changed, the salesperson revisits all the details with the buyer, not just impact and critical event, but also the creation of a 3x3:

- Three people on your team each work with a different person on their team
- Then, have people from your team reach out to people on their team
- This may involve sales ghostwriting the first message

Step 3. Kick-off

- Send a brief welcome note, which may include some kind of an icebreaker
- Create the impact journey that defines by when a specific impact should be achieved
- Obtain the dates of the client's monthly internal executive meetings
- Establish the cadence of *scheduled events*, such as the renewal date and its conditions
- Set alerts for *triggered events*, such as opportunities and/or risks, and define the actions you will take on each alert

MOMENT #6: ENSURE IMPACT IS ACHIEVED, NOT USAGE

Many organizations track product use as an indicator of how well the product is doing and how healthy the account is. Whether measured in terms of percentage of seats used or number of logins per time period or number of features used, know that product usage is the *proxy* for success – it is not the success itself . . . ironic, because what the software measures is not customer success, but rather the product's success. A more impact-focused approach would be to explore whether the customer is getting the results they need out of the product – which may or may not correlate with product usage. After all, from a customer's standpoint, what could be better than solving their pain with the minimum amount of product usage possible?

Of course, it's often the case that more usage will solve the problem, in which case, usage is a reasonable proxy for impact. But it is important to keep CSMs and account managers focused on the fact that the customer is buying *impact*, not usage.

What is more important to a customer is a frequent report that shows the results or impact they had sought. For example, during the orchestration meeting, you can establish a 12-month impact plan. At the same time, you can agree to report monthly on the impact achieved, along with suggested corrective actions for improvement.

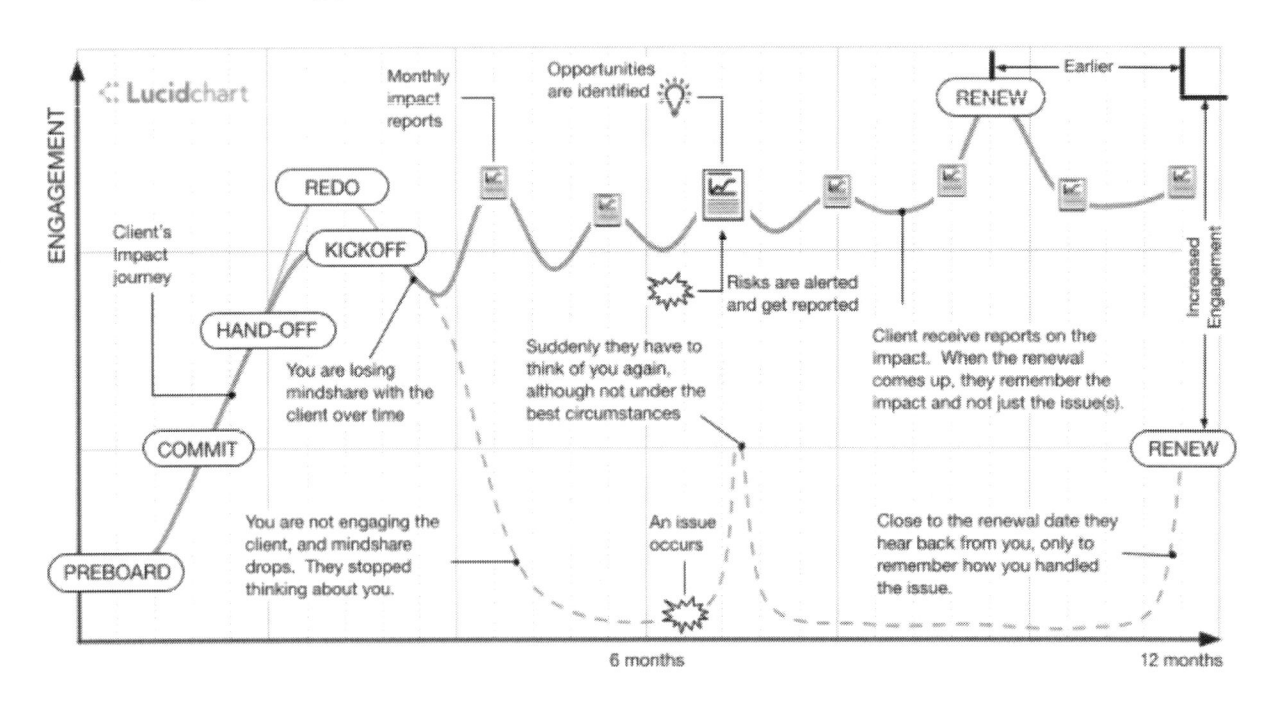

Figure 6.6 The importance of frequent impact reports vs. a quarterly business review

Case in point: Many consider the quarterly business review, or QBR, one of the key meetings with the stakeholders inside a company. This causes a problem, because the number of SaaS software vendors for a 500-person company ranges somewhere between 50 to 100! If each of them required a one-hour QBR, it would take weeks of meetings with vendors every quarter to discuss usage of each of these products.

It's okay to only have other meetings scheduled, such as the orchestration/kick off and the renewal call, but monthly impact reports should also be sent in lieu of a QBR.

Blueprint 6.6a Establish an impact journey

Step 1. Orchestrate a road to help the customer achieve their desired impact

Step 2. Practice how to handle frustration when an issue occurs:

- Communicate: Establish a solid way of communicating (e.g., "TALKER")
- Disarm: Express empathy/disarm the situation, without taking on blame
- Research: Important to find relevant evidence and data points; do not diagnose without this!
- Diagnose: Perform a proper diagnosis based on the research
- Proof: Before you prescribe, summarize the proof of your case
- Prescribe: Recommend based on research/diagnosis/proof
- Communicate: Summarize, and then offer help to implement

Step 3. Provide a *scheduled report* every month that clearly indicates the impact that has been achieved:

- The report must have an easy-to-understand chart visualizing the impact
- Include the achieved emotional and rational impacts
- Present a benchmark of their impact achieved vs. others in the industry
- Include risks and opportunities, with thoughtful observations
- Always look forward 6-12 months, regardless of the renewal date

Step 4. Renew and expand the contract well before the actual renewal due date; the renewal should be based on the emotional and rational impact provided to a client, not just the usage.

MOMENT #7: GROW THE IMPACT

"Land and Expand" has been a buzzword in SaaS marketing circles. It's a useful metaphor with its beachheads and advances. But it is a metaphor rooted in conflict. It sees the customer as a territory to be mapped, flanked, and conquered. It is reasonable to assume that this is *not* how the customer views the relationship. Instead, we advise expansion teams, usually under the responsibility of account managers (AMs), to think about growing the relationship and growing the customer's business. This can only be achieved by having an impact. Whether that impact is lower cost, higher revenue, or an improved customer experience, it is the impact that matters to the customer, and the more impact delivered, the more the customer will want to use the product and expand the relationship as well.

Expanding the impact or growing the business is a function of two factors: Impact and Benefactor. For example, when an existing client renews their contract and wants more of the same impact, it is referred to as a renewal. Often these renewals occur automatically on the renewal date. In many cases, the CSM is responsible for this. This is a flawed approach, as you ignore the growth potential from a client who may be willing to renew only nine months into a contract.

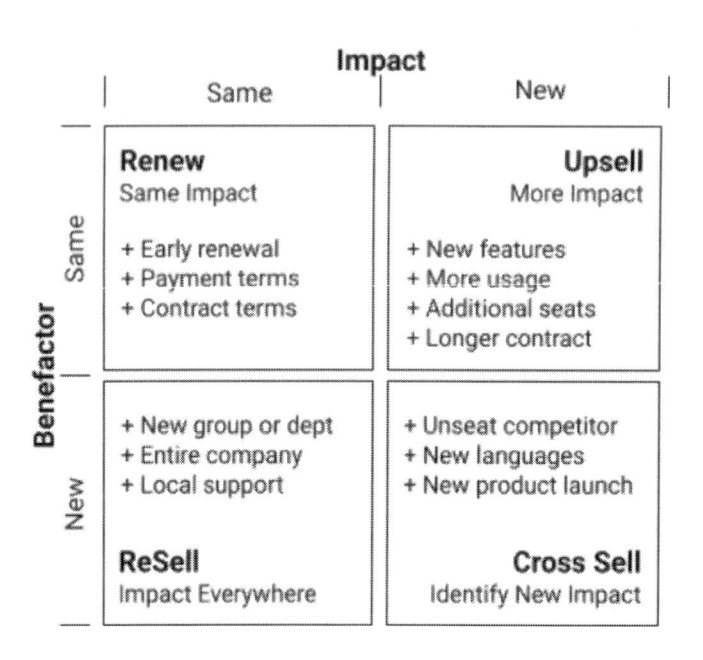

	Impact: Same	Impact: New
Benefactor: Same	**Renew** — Same Impact + Early renewal + Payment terms + Contract terms	**Upsell** — More Impact + New features + More usage + Additional seats + Longer contract
Benefactor: New	**ReSell** — Impact Everywhere + New group or dept + Entire company + Local support	**Cross Sell** — Identify New Impact + Unseat competitor + New languages + New product launch

Figure 6.7a Four growth areas, each with their own opportunity

However, when an existing client buys more services, such as more seats or additional features, this is considered an upsell. CSMs are capable of doing this reactively - but if you want to reach out proactively, you are likely going to need an acquisition-focused salesforce.

When a new benefactor in an existing account needs to be won over, this is referred to as a cross-sell. A cross-sell should never be handled by a CSM, as this is the most complicated sale, and you may need to unroot an existing competitor chosen by another champion. This is often better handled by a team familiar with competing, such as the acquisitions team.

As outlined in Figure 6.7b, there are four growth areas, each with their own specific goal that loop back into different parts of the process.

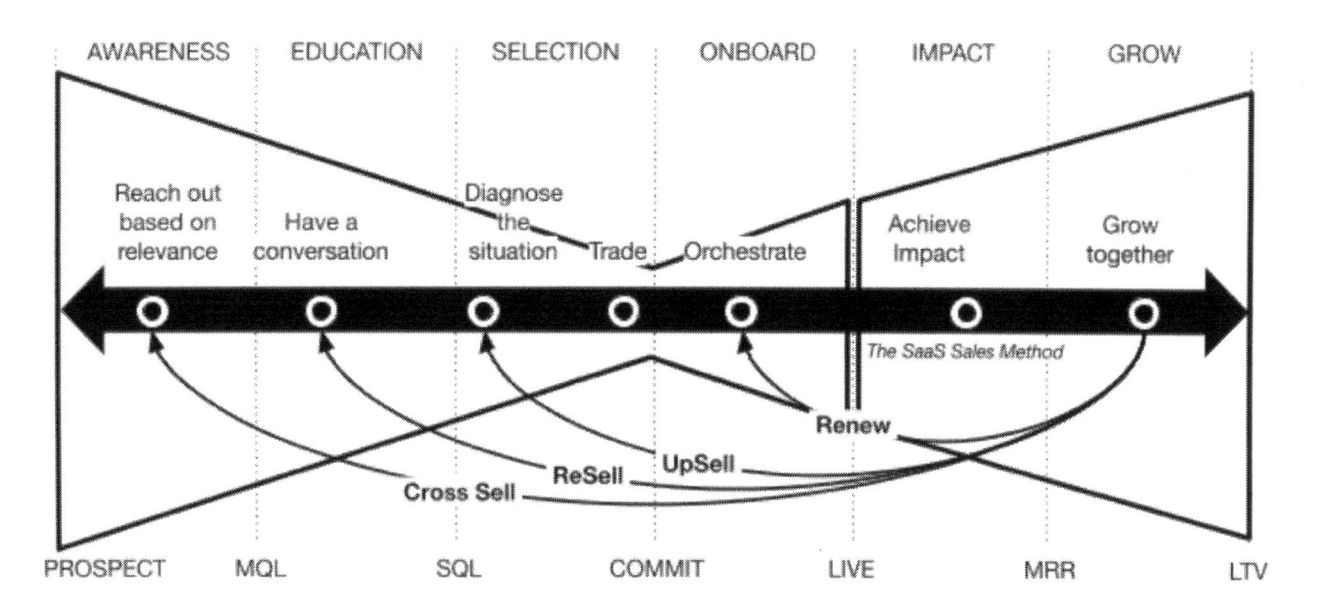

Figure 6.7b Growth opportunities mapped back to key Moments, creating growth loops

Blueprint 6.7 Establish an impact journey

Step 1. Create a 2 x 2 table with the four growth areas outlined below.

Step 2. Assign each area to the right person in your organization. For example:

- Renewal of the contract ⇒ Customer Success Manager
- Upsell to a new product ⇒ Sales or Account Management
- Resell to a new a new benefactor ⇒ Sales or Account Management
- Cross-sell to a new benefactor ⇒ Account Management

Step 3. Determine the growth conditions in each area. For example, under renewal when impact is achieved, there are still various growth opportunities:

- Annual x% increase in price
- Renew earlier, e.g., 9 months into a 12-month contract
- Extend contract terms from a 12-month to a 24-month contract

Step 4. Create a blueprint for each of these growth areas, addressing the most common scenarios.

Step 5. Practice performing these actions with the team! Do not do this with a customer without having practiced and role-played the most common scenarios.

BONUS MOMENT: STAGING OF MEETINGS

Most business today is the result of a series of meetings, with the quality of each meeting determining how many meetings you need to achieve your end goal. We've found that successful sales people have fewer and shorter meetings.

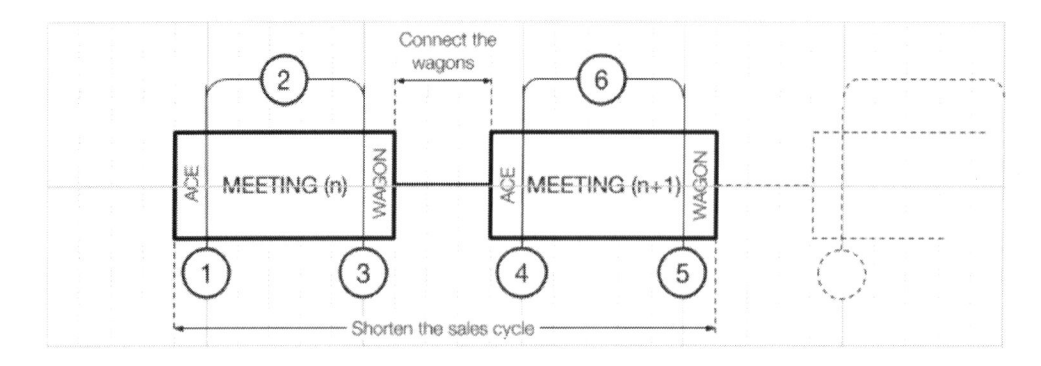

Figure 6.8 How to stage meetings to achieve the goal and shorten the sales cycle

By reviewing tens of thousands of sales meetings, both in person and on the phone, we've found that great meetings follow a consistent blueprint:

Blueprint 6.8 Staging the meetings using ACE and WAGONs

Step 1. **ACE** the meeting. Check the end-time and set the end goal of the meeting:

- **Appreciation**: Appreciate you taking the time to meet today.
- **Check time**: Are we still good till 11am?
- **End goal**: This is an introductory call to see if we can help you. If yes, we normally move forward with a demonstration. Does that sound right?

Step 2. Present an agenda to *meet the end goal* and ask the customers to contribute:

- What would you like to discuss today?

Step 3. At the end of the meeting, ask if the goals were met:

- May I ask, based on what we discussed today, do you think we can help you?

Step 4. If so, confirm that the client is ready to move forward:

- Are you ready to move forward with a demonstration?

The next part is critical to link to the outcome of the next meeting:

Step 5. Set the stage for the next meeting:

- Have you done similar demos like this before?
- What has been the outcome of a successful demo in the past?

Step 6. There are three ways to get the right people in the room to achieve the end goal.

Ask with an open-ended question:

- Is there anyone else who can benefit from attending this demo?

Ask with a close-ended question:

- Mary is your head of Sales Ops, right? Do you think she can benefit from attending the demo?

Ask with a third-party reference:

- I recently did a demo with {{first name}}, she is one of your peers and decided to bring in her head of Sales Ops to address the integration with your CRM. I notice Mary is your head of Sales Ops. Do you think she can benefit from joining us?

Regardless of the outcome, you can always follow through:

- Since Mary can/can't join us today, what does she normally care about?

RECAP CHAPTER 6 | **BLUEPRINTS**

To impact change, we recommend the following steps:

Step 1. Identify the key Moments for your business

Step 2. Measure the conversion metric and maintain a trendline over time

Step 3. Determine the actions performed during a key Moment, and visualize them in a blueprint

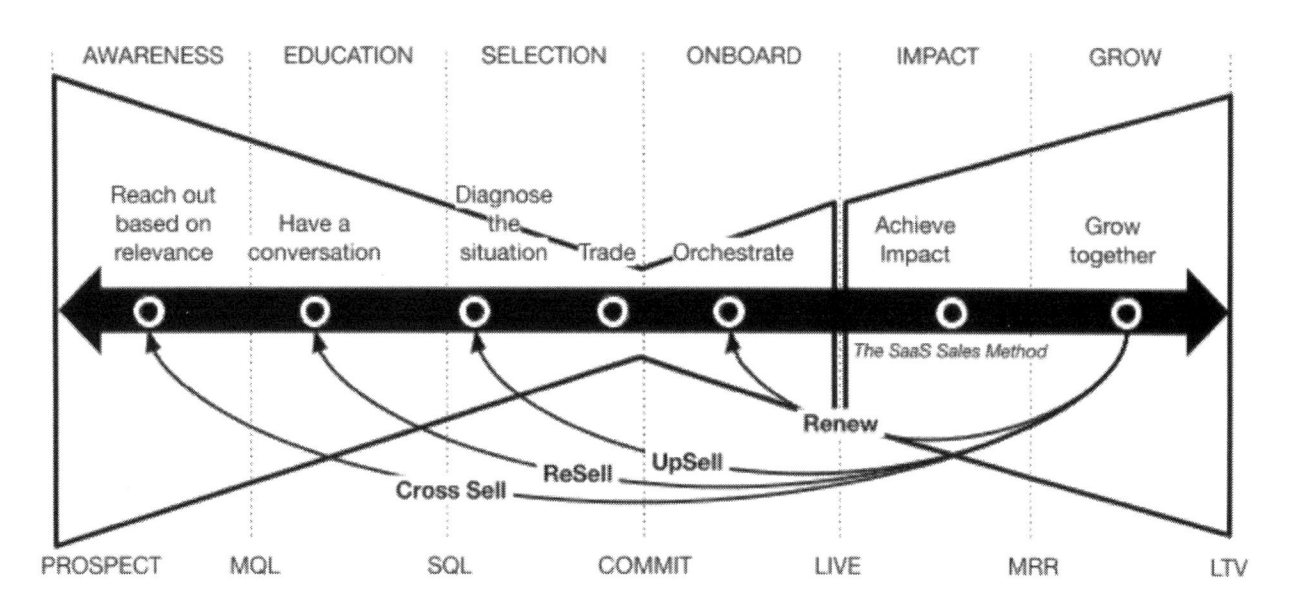

Step 4. Brainstorm how each key Moment can be improved

Step 5. Iterate in 15- to 30-day intervals until you have improved the metric by 10%

Step 6. Benchmark your performance against others relevant to your business

CHAPTER 7
HOW TO KEEP GOING

Implementing a process-driven sales method is not easy. It requires patience, deliberateness, and long term thinking. We know these are not the traits of your average sales team! But as selling evolves into more of a science and less of an art, making the investment will pay off in the form of predictability, scalability, and ultimately customer impact. Similarly, talking about fundamental skills isn't as sexy as, say, a LinkedIn hack that gets everyone to open your outbound email for a short period of time. We strongly believe, though, that teaching everyone in your organization who faces the customer to think ahead and structure their approach, as well as deliberate in what and how they communicate, will pay massive dividends over time.

Indeed, that cumulative effect of applying fundamental skills in the Moments that Matter to the customer is exceedingly more powerful and sustainable than most of us recognize! Regardless of whether you choose to implement the whole SaaS Sales Method, we've seen over and over again how powerful it is to get those fundamental skills right.

Lastly, process thinking is alien to most sales leaders, but the process revolutions that have transformed manufacturing, logistics, and most other sectors of the economy through iterative improvement can do the same in sales. We've seen it happen. The most savvy revenue leaders completely buy into the idea that Sales as a Science is the next step in the development of the modern revenue organization. What is harder to convey is that implementing a scientific approach requires a change in culture rather than a change in people. The common instinct to replace people rather than fix process is, after all, the very essence of the 'person culture' we are trying to replace!

That said, the easiest way for companies looking to adopt a scientific approach to make significant changes is by focusing on fundamental skills like communication and meeting management during the Moments that Matter. Marginal improvement in the Moments that Matter can mean doing things differently from how they are normally done - but the payoff at the systems level is multiplicative, not additive!

Now - *and this is very important* - unlike manufacturing, where once a process is stable and yielding well, your goal is to control and keep the process steady, the opportunity for performance improvement in sales never stops! Competitors change, your team changes, and customer requirements change. This makes process improvement in sales a continuous and iterative process.

Step-by-Step Program

Step 1. Get buy-in from the top. This program requires not just executive buy-in, but more importantly, executive involvement. We have found the best way is a one-day workshop with all customer-facing roles, such as marketing, sales, customer success, and even product management, present to discuss. Sample agenda:

- Data Model: What are we measuring? Definitions and criteria?
- Growth Plan: What are the growth aspirations over the next two years? What is the growth model and the growth formula based on the business?
- The SaaS Sales Methodology: Are we aligned on the same methodology?
- Moments That Matter: What are the moments that matter most to our customers?
- Data Driven: Where are we now on each key Moment?
- Blueprinting: How to create a blueprint for each Moment and improve by 10%?

Step 2. Establish a data model. As outlined in Chapter 4, establish a model. A good time to do this is right when you have achieved product market fit, and you are anticipating growth from different markets, products, and/or regions.

Step 3. Obtain the data. Measure the conversion rates (CR1 to CR7) and timelines (T1 to T7) for each of the seven key Moments in your business, and then benchmark those metrics against others who are relevant within your market.

ACV	CR1	CR2	CR3	CR4	T4	CR5	CR6	CR7
SMB: _____								
MID: _____								
ENT: _____								

Step 4. Find the Moments that Matter. Identify your best customers, and then do a search in your email on that customer's domain name, and look at the

activity on those accounts in your CRM. Use this information to identify the journey the customer took, and map that against the key Moments:

- How did the relationship start?
- What was discussed in the first call, the first meeting?
- Who helped the process?
- What was the impact and the critical event?
- What did they end up using?
- How is it currently impacting their business?

Step 5. **Blueprint each Moment.** Design the ideal experience, using the blueprints we have provided in this book as an example.

Step 6. **Enable and train.** Provide your teams with the knowledge, content, tools, and organizational structure to execute the process.

- Skills: Instead of one or two full training days, we recommend that you perform frequent training. Learning should be broken up into 10% training, 20% peer exercises, and 70% practice in the field using a monthly/weekly/daily program.
- Tools: Tools have to act as a force multiplier. They cannot just operate as a management tool to measure performance.
- Enablement: The team must have a library of insightful content they can share with the client based on the current stage.
- Organization: We recommend a flat and agile structure based on merit, not seniority.

Step 7. **Implementation.** Note that implementation is the application of trained skills to real life scenarios. We recommend call analytics tools to ensure that the content is correctly implemented. As you implement, make small adjustments until you get it right, and be sure to use a subset of the team to perform an A/B test.

Step 8. **Assessment.** Measure the results along the same model. Did you achieve the desired impact? Share your experience with the team. What worked and what did not work? It sounds simple, but do more of what works and stop doing what doesn't work.

This is a continuous improvement process; this means that even if you achieved the desired outcome, you still can go deeper on a specific metric and improve it by a few percentage points. Pick one key performance indicator each quarter to improve.

Enable Your Team

To enable your team, we have provided a series of textbooks via Amazon containing dozens of blueprints for every part of your organization:

Develop Skills

To train your team, we offer a series of options: individual training via our open classes, or dedicated custom training, where organizations can plug this framework into their existing sales methodology and continue to leverage the investment in any previous sales method.

We hope to have given you lots of ideas to fill you with excitement, provide you with a beautiful purpose, and see that there is as much science to working with clients as there is art.

APPENDIX
A FEW HELPFUL TOOLS

APPENDIX A QUALIFICATION METHODOLOGIES

There is a common confusion between sales methodologies and qualification methodologies.

One of the earliest qualification methods is BANT (Budget, Authority, Need, and Timeline of the decision). It originates from sales teams at IBM who, during the 1960s and 1970s, used BANT to recognize real buyers for their truck-size, mainframe computers versus those who just wanted to see a demo. In today's world, this method facilitates a solution sell.

There are several other qualification methods out there, such as ANUM and CHAMP. The latter differs by focusing on identifying challenges, and starts to line up with consultative selling (as opposed to solution selling). FAINT, where sellers provoke interest, lines up with provocative selling; MEDDIC, created by Dick Dunkel and Jack Napoli during the 1990s, focuses on the impact to a client's business as well as the decision process.

There is no qualification method that is better or worse, but we advise the teams that we consult for to ensure that they are not applying a method to the wrong situation. For example, using BANT in a provocative first call is doomed for failure. And putting a client who is ready to buy through MEDDIC is unlikely to yield a satisfactory result.

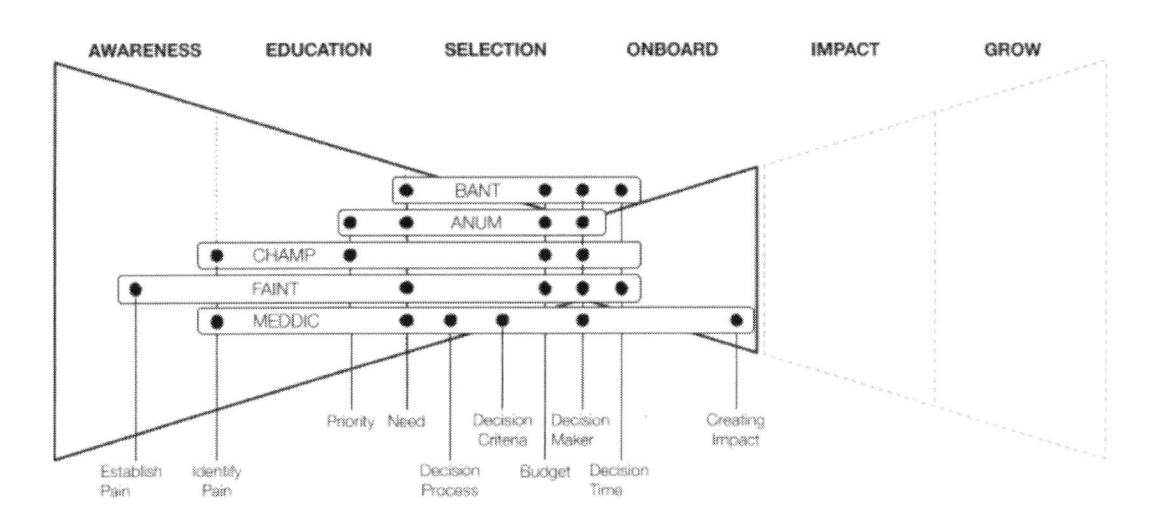

Figure A.1 Comparison of qualification methodologies

APPENDIX B THE INEFFICIENCY OF A ONE-STAGE ORGANIZATION

Between approximately $10,000 to $40,000 ACV, there is a strong benefit to using a 2-stage sales organization. A 2-stage organization is made up of two key roles: sales development reps (SDRs) who arrange meetings with the account executives (AEs) performing the sales calls. The figure below depicts the activities an AE has to do if they do it by themselves.

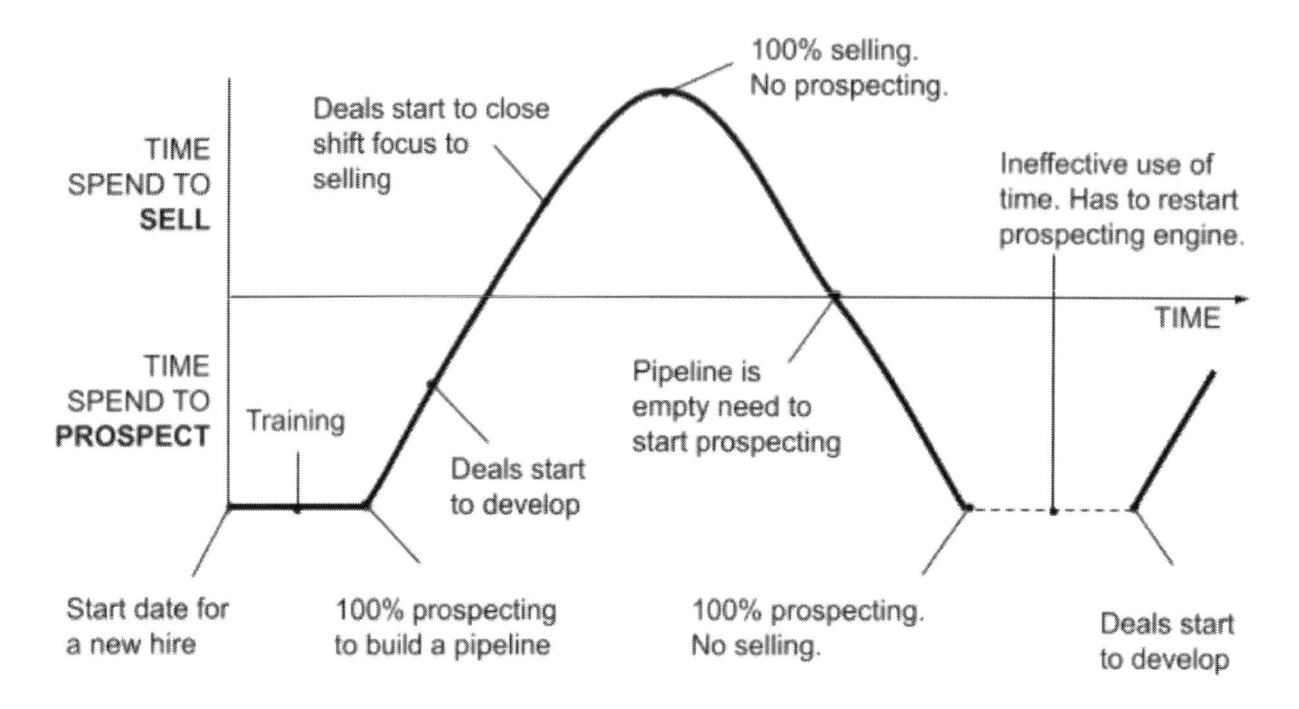

Figure B.1 Ineffective use of time by a 1-stage organization

The efficiency and effectiveness of an organization is primarily in a narrow window between an ACV of $10,000 and $40,000. If you are within this range with your ACV, you should investigate the effectiveness and efficiency of your AE doing both prospecting and selling. Having the AE doing both jobs while you are in this window results in:

- **Longer sales cycles:** Unless you have a lot of inbound, the AE will need to reload the funnel after a busy selling cycle, such as the last week of the month/quarter; it is very unlikely for sales people to maintain a healthy balance between prospecting and winning, as their incentives are skewed towards selling.
- **Hero-to-Zero:** As salespeople reload, you may experience fluctuating performance from the AE, literally going from being on target to missing it by fifty percent. This is the result of restarting the prospecting engine subsequent to every selling cycle.

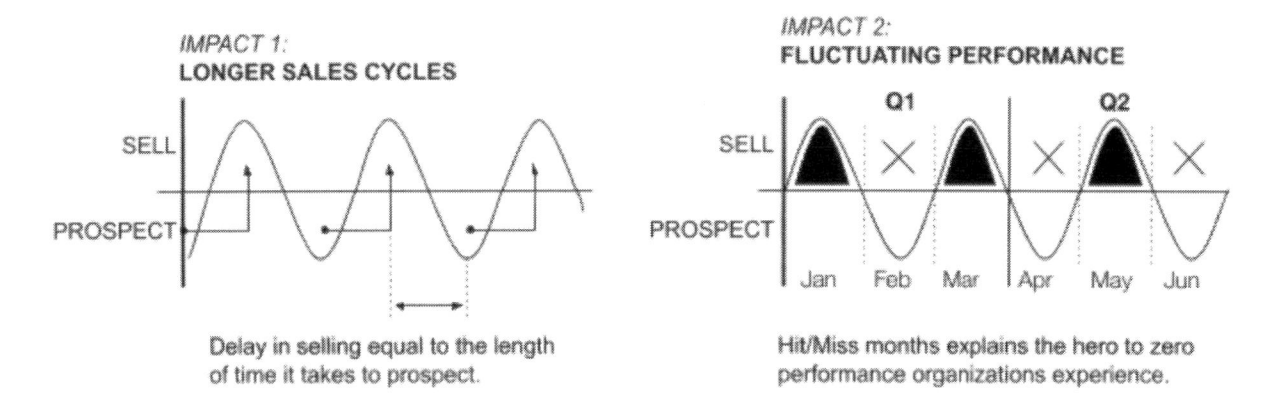

Figure B.2 Impact of a 1-stage sales cycle

What to do outside this window?

- **On the low-end** of this spectrum, you are limited by efficiency. A two-stage model in this scenario simply costs too much money to acquire the revenue. Instead, we recommend that you automate as much as possible. As soon as you are below an ACV of $5,000, you will likely be forced to rely on an inbound-only machine.
- **At the high end** of this spectrum, your performance is limited by effectiveness due to the buying complexity. Selling solutions over $40,000 are complex enough that most SDRs will lack the knowledge required to have a meaningful conversation with a buyer who, at this price, is likely a senior executive.

Regardless, we highly recommend that you calculate the cost of the acquisition of a group of customers. If your cost of the SDR, AE, and Onboarder exceed 40% of the annual revenues produced, you may have to change your go-to-market strategy (or if you are selling multi-year contracts, this can be closer to 50%).

APPENDIX C JOB DESCRIPTIONS

To help you get started, we have included a sample job description for a Revenue Ops/Sales Strategist:

You are the "chief of staff" of the revenue organization, helping to drive sales effectiveness and sales efficiency. You're hands-on in defining and instrumenting everything about the sales process and sales organization, analyzing data to find opportunities for improvement, and working to move the needle on key performance indicators each month.

This position has high visibility with the CEO and board of directors. It is a leadership position where you work cross-functionally to define and improve the process and implement training and coaching. You will recommend and oversee new enablement programs, organizational structure, and compensation plans.

Project Management and Stakeholder Management:

- Help us imagine, via data, how to continuously evolve and de-risk every component of our business
- Communicate and coordinate with other team leads and business leadership to ensure appropriate integration of processes across the organization
- Drive the design and implementation of new business processes with organizational structure and required CRM configuration; must be able to coordinate across teams to align operations toward stated goals
- Functional understanding of CRM capabilities including integrations with various systems
- Board-level report creation, analysis, and administration

Continuous Improvement:

- Supports the ongoing development (and phased releases) of CRM as a sales, marketing, support, and management tool
- Engages key stakeholders (Executive, Support, Sales, Marketing, IT, Product, etc.) for timely and meaningful feedback to leverage the information for better system adoption and enhancements
- Drives for process effectiveness at each and every level of the organization; applies consistent global processes

Specific Job Skills:

- Relates well to all personality types inside and outside the organization; builds appropriate rapport and uses diplomacy and tact
- Solid verbal and written presentation, communication, and influencing skills; can work across multiple countries and cultures
- Strong problem solving, analytical and troubleshooting skills, with the ability to exercise mature judgment
- Must possess solid judgment and ability to work autonomously from established goals and strategic direction; must be able to cope with ambiguity
- Possess strategic thinking, and can look ahead and respond proactively
- Possess change management and leadership skills; demonstrates ability to effect change on a global scale
- Ability to work in a complex matrix environment to create buy-in and implement processes
- Demonstrated experience with CRM vendor selection process; experience with CRM specifications, vendor RFQ and integration assessments.

Qualifications:

- 3-5 years business operations and project management experience
- Analytical thinker
- At least one year CRM experience
- Understanding of the tech industry and SaaS business models
- Ability to manage and lead a team

APPENDIX D REFERENCES

TITLE	AUTHOR(S)
Accelerate	John P. Kotter
Aligning Strategy & Sales	Frank Cespedes
Beautiful Evidence	Edward R. Tufte
Blueprints for a SaaS Sales Organization	Jacco van der Kooij & Fernando Pizarro
Building Trust, Growing Sales	Daniel J. Adams
Challenger Selling	Matt Dixon & Brent Adamson
Cracking the Sales Management Code	Jason Jordan
Design to Test	Jon Torino & Frank Binnendyk
Exceptional Selling	Jeff Thull
Farm Not Hunt	Guy Nirpaz & Fernando Pizarro
Gemba Kaizen	Masaaki Imai
Getting More	Stuart Diamond
Human Error: Models and Management	James Reason
In a Downturn Provoke Your Customer	Philip Lay, Todd Hewlin, Geoffrey Moore
Let's Get Real or Let's Not Play	Mahan Khalsa & Randy Illig
Major Account Strategy	Neil Rackham
Managing Major Sales	Neil Rackham & Richard Ruff
Mastering the Complex Sales	Jeff Thull
Moneyball, The Art of Winning an Unfair Game	Michael Lewis
Power of Habit	Charles Duhigg
Rethinking the Salesforce	Neil Rackham & John De Vincentis
SaaS Metrics 2.0	David Skok
Secret of Question Based Selling	Eric Freese
Secrets of Closing the Sale	Zig Ziglar
Selling is a Team Sport	Eric Baron
Spin Selling	Neil Rackham
Survival to Thrival	Bob Tinker & Tae Hea Nahm
The Concept of Diminishing Returns	Jakob Nielsen
The Decision Book	Mikael Krogerus & Roman Tschäppeler
The New Solution Selling	Keith Eades
The Sales Acceleration Formula	Mark Roberge
The Startup Owner's Manual	Steve Blank & Bob Dorf
To Sell is Human	Daniel H. Pink
Universal Principles of Design	William Lidwell, Kritina Holden, Jill Butler

Printed in Poland
by Amazon Fulfillment
Poland Sp. z o.o., Wrocław
04 October 2022

b7af4f86-9753-4e8e-8fd5-5630a9fce7f9R01